Davey

Thanks for your

demonstration of leadership

Love Charlee

Participative Management
Implementing Empowerment

Participative Management
Implementing Empowerment

Lorne C. Plunkett
Robert Fournier

John Wiley & Sons, Inc.
New York • Chichester • Brisbane • Toronto • Singapore

In recognition of the importance of preserving what has been
written, it is a policy of John Wiley & Sons, Inc., to have
books of enduring value published in the United States
printed on acid-free paper, and we exert our best efforts
to that end.

This publication is designed to provide accurate and
authoritative information in regard to the subject
matter covered. It is sold with the understanding that
the publisher is not engaged in rendering legal, accounting,
or other professional services. If legal advice or other
expert assistance is required, the services of a competent
professional person should be sought. *From a Declaration
of Principles jointly adopted by a Committee of the
American Bar Association and a Committee of Publishers.*

Library of Congress Cataloging-in-Publication Data

Plunkett, Lorne C.
    Participative management : implementing
empowerment / by Lorne Plunkett and Robert Fournier.
        p.   cm.
    Includes bibliographical references.
    ISBN 0-471-54374-8 (cloth : alk. paper)
    1. Industrial management—Employee participation. I. Fournier.
R. O.   II. Title.
HD5650.P537 1991
658.3'152—dc20   91-15588

Printed in the United States of America

10 9 8 7 6 5 4 3 2 1

PREFACE

WHO SHOULD READ THIS BOOK?

We wrote this book hoping that leaders, supervisors, hourly
paid workers, and employee representatives (e.g., union stew-
ards) all would benefit from reading it. We wrote it primarily
with those people in mind because they are the ones who will
experience the participative management process as both a
personal and an organizational event. We also hope that internal and external change agents—whether they be organization
development consultants or trainers—will gain value from our
experiences. The change agent is helpful or not, depending on
what processes or programs are recommended to the clients.
For practitioners, our message is simply to ask, "If I was paying
the bill for my services, would I feel that I was spending my
organization's money effectively?"

OVERVIEW OF THE CONTENTS

Chapter 1 provides an overview of participative management
from our perspective. We also describe a case with which we
have been associated that exemplifies the concept and practice
of participative management and reinforces our belief that the
process pays off organizationally. In Chapter 2, we attempt to
demystify what we view as the "top ten" myths of participative
management. We explore the traps associated with the myths
and try to illustrate the impact of subscribing to them.

Chapter 3 addresses the issues for the organization in the participative management process. Chapter 4 explores issues for teams and groups. Chapter 5 offers some techniques that we have found useful in working with varieties of teams we have encountered in the participative management process.

In Chapter 6, we discuss issues for the individuals in the participative management process, which we too often find are simply not addressed. In this chapter, we write of the "unspeakables" because we believe that to ignore them is to ignore the very foundation on which participative management is built.

Chapter 7 attempts to look into the future and predict where participative management is going.

The Appendixes in this book are intentionally different from many other appendixes. We seized the opportunity to turn the book into a working document of sorts. We offer some tools that have worked for others, some examples of successful pieces in the participative management process, and a list of reference books that we found especially useful in our work with clients.

ACKNOWLEDGMENTS

For many years, we talked about the collaborating for this book. In 1990, we put the plan in progress, and in doing so we experienced some of the same successes and failures that we describe in this book. We have certainly increased our empathy toward our clients as they struggle with participative management issues. In the end, however, we persisted and the feeling of completion is empowering! The book was written in two different cities (we live 400 miles apart), and we had to invent some creative ways to apply teamwork in our efforts to meet deadlines. We owe an incredible debt to the inventors of the telephone, the fax machine, and the courier service.

We wrote this book for a number of reasons. First, we felt a strong need to share our own experiences, beliefs, and concerns about participative management and how it is "done." Second, we believed that if we could marry our "internal–external" consulting perceptions, we could come up with a clearer view of participative management concepts and techniques. Third, our spouses suggested we should either write the book or stop talking about it!

You can't write a book like this without help and support from a lot of people. We want to acknowledge all of our clients, particularly the following who allowed us to share their experiences: the polyvinyl chloride expansion team at Esso Chemical Canada's Sarnia site, Shell Canada, Camco, Nova's Polysar site, General Electric Canada, Peterborough, and Martin Marietta, Denver.

ACKNOWLEDGMENTS

Special thanks from Bob to Bill Dyer and Bob Tannenbaum, whose words of experience and wisdom to the Pepperdine class were inspirational and clarifying at a time when both were needed most.

Special thanks from Lorne to colleagues at Lorne Plunkett & Associates Ltd. and the clients who have become friends for reading drafts and sharing their insights. Lorne particularly thanks Mike Hamilton, our editor, from John Wiley for his patience and support of our efforts.

Three other people were instrumental in helping write this book. Diane Plunkett and Debbie Fournier, whose third-party interventions got us going again at critical points in the writing process, and Pam Whitty, whose skill in transforming our different writing styles to legibly typed pages, and in keeping us coordinated and on track, helped enormously.

CONTENTS

CONTENTS

CONTENTS

1

INTRODUCTION

IF PARTICIPATIVE MANAGEMENT IS THE ANSWER, WHAT WAS THE QUESTION?

Have you been on a trip when you had to refer to maps and checkpoints so constantly that you asked yourself, "Why did I undertake this journey?" This same feeling is probably rampant in organizations undertaking the shift in management philosophy to participative management. We consistently meet managers who are checking progress, mapping out tactics, confronting detours, and trying to keep the "kids in the backseat quiet." What started out as a "grand journey" is becoming a "never-to-be-repeated experience." This book is not meant to be a travel guide for visiting the world of participative management. Instead, it is meant to provide some *working* answers that might reduce the anxiety intrinsic to making a necessary and challenging business decision.

In this book, we want to provide you with a different slant to participative management. Most of the literature in the field is "missionary" in nature, extolling the benefits of a new way of working. They make promises to managers of a nirvana that is hard to ignore. We maintain that reality is the road to nirvana, and this book is about reality. We intend to share our experiences—both the failures and the successes. Our clients have allowed us to discuss their experiences in the hopes that other managers will either avoid some of the pitfalls or not feel that they alone have moments of doubt.

This is not a negative book. We believe deeply in the philosophy of participative management. However, good intentions alone are not enough to achieve success.

WHAT MAKES THIS BOOK DIFFERENT?

Several features make this book different:

1. We focus on the individual in an organization. Participative management cannot be successful if there is not a proper reconciliation of the individual's needs and the organization's need to change.

2. We emphasize the difficulties faced in a move to participative management. Managers cannot fight a battle without being aware of the battlefield.

3. We provide no panacea. Creating a challenging and fulfilling workplace is not as simple as many consultants would like managers to believe. There is no *one* right way. Success is based on using a wide range of strategies to get to a clearly defined end point.

4. We introduce participative management as a "business decision." Our approach is simple: "Don't do participative management for your employees' sake; do it for the business' sake. We believe the purpose is business stability and growth, not employee fulfillment. Participation is a means, not an end.

WHAT IS PARTICIPATIVE MANAGEMENT?

Although the literature of management abounds with definitions of participative management, we could not find a satisfactory definition. In our view, participative management is a philosophy that demands that organizational decision making be made in such a way that *input* and *responsibility* are extended to the lowest level appropriate to the decision being made.

The purpose of participative management is to ensure that effective decisions are made by the right people. Empowerment is a means to achieve participative management. It is the mechanism by which responsibility is vested in teams or individuals. Involvement, on the other hand, is the mechanism for ensuring appropriate input to decision making. Thus, empowerment and involvement become the building blocks for a participative management philosophy.

Throughout this book, the concept of teams plays an important part. Consistent with our definition of participative management, teams are another tool in the participative management toolbox. Although teams are critical for participative management, they are not participative management by themselves. If a team is created but not consulted or empowered, participative management will not exist. Many writers and practicing consultants tend to use football or hockey teams as effective analogies for participative management. We have a small problem with this. Football and hockey assume that everyone is involved in every play. Each player on the field or ice surface has a totally interdependent role with everyone else. In business, however, this is not necessarily true. Very few teams are so integrated that true interdependence is required. Baseball seems to be a better example for understanding teams in a participative management philosophy. In baseball, although there is definitely a need for role specialization and goal clarity, it is not uncommon for a left fielder to go three or four innings and never touch the ball. The game goes on, but the left fielder has little, if any ability to influence the course of events. What is critical for the team is that when the left fielder *is* needed, he or she is ready to carry out the designated responsibilities.

Participative management is more like baseball in that each individual is not involved in every decision in the organization, but is required to be effective when his or her input is required. Participative management also requires that the organization and its leadership recognize when to involve people and when to let them get on with running the business. Many of these issues are covered in later chapters.

WHY PARTICIPATIVE MANAGEMENT?

Every organization moves to participative management for its own reasons. However, there seem to be two recurring themes:

1. Sharing success rather than hoarding failure. The traditional methods of management are inefficient for many organizations. Many companies are seeing market share and size diminish due to loss of quality standards, increasing militancy of an unhappy workforce, or a competitor's increased effectiveness. In considering solutions, many companies focus on the Japanese philosophy. Roger Smith, chief executive officer of General Motors, believed that the lesson to be learned from the Japanese was robotics. Xerox opted for customer service as its main competitive response. Ford has taken the philosophy that "quality is job one." All these strategies include some form of participative management as part of the total solution. Increasing business effectiveness is *impossible* without increasing the effectiveness of the human resources in the company. Participative management provides an opportunity to share responsibility, risk, and success. The old days of the heroic leader who battles impossible odds on behalf of his or her people are over. Organizations know that sharing the responsibility with

everyone involved is a powerful antidote for complacency and failure.

2. The emergence of the knowledge worker. The last 20 years have seen a dramatic change in the requirements for the workforce in industry and business. Peter Drucker coined the phrase "knowledge worker" in the late 1970s. He described the change occurring in the technology of companies that caused a switch from manual labor to technical knowledge and analytical thinking skills. In a refinery today, two people can sit at a control board and monitor two acres of equipment. Although people are still needed, the company requires different things from its people.

With this change in the roles and expectations of employees comes a realization that today's average worker represents a valuable resource in terms of the business. In the 1950s and 1960s, the value of workers was measured in terms of dependability, physical strength, experience, and loyalty. Today, we want innovation, acceptance of responsibility, and customer focus. Participative management becomes a way of using this changed resource for the organization. It unleashes the knowledge and skills of those people who do the job.

PARTICIPATIVE MANAGEMENT AT ESSO CHEMICAL CANADA

The following story illustrates why participative management is important. We hope that this story, which describes a real team in a real plant, provides an impetus for you to delve further into participative management and learn how it was done—successfully. In 1987, Esso Chemical Canada decided to expand its polyvinyl chloride (PVC) facility at Sarnia, Ontario.

The expansion was intended to increase the plant's production capacity from 90 thousand tons to 120 thousand tons per year. The expansion decision in and of itself was not startling or innovative; however, Esso's approach to designing and constructing the expansion was a clear departure from previous expansions. It represents a positive model of participative management.

Traditional Approach

Traditionally, a project of this nature is carried out as follows:

1. An engineering group of internal and external engineers designs the expansion based on some well-defined engineering standards. This usually takes place away from the plant, and input is scarce.

2. Once the design phase is completed, the design is handed over to a construction crew, usually an external contractor. At this point, the designers are usually reassigned, having completed their job.

3. As construction nears completion, the partially completed plant is handed over to the internal maintenance department. Their job is to fix things that are not right. If major problems in design or construction are found, all the feedback is given to the project engineers, and very little data ever reach the designers.

This is a fairly standard approach to building or expanding plants of this nature. We are not criticizing the process, because it usually works fairly efficiently. In the end, the plants run as intended, give or take a few glitches.

Participative Management Approach

Engineers made up the initial Esso PVC expansion team of 1988. They invited a process operator to join the team's discussions as they tried to organize and develop a basis for the expansion. These discussions led to the conclusion that the team did not have the proper membership. Members agreed that, to carry out the project effectively, they would require the involvement of operating, maintenance, and quality control people. According to Brian Procunier, the senior project engineer, "We didn't make a conscious decision to involve those folks up front; we evolved to it as a logical way to go." As they struggled with the issue, the engineers identified a number of benefits of using a high-involvement process. First, the engineers would learn the plant operating process, which would give them more influence over details and the construction phase. Second, in the construction phase, they would be better able to provide effective answers to operating people about why and how certain things were being built. Third, they would have more direct knowledge of all aspects of the project.

At this point, operating, maintenance, and quality control representatives were invited to join the team and become full members in the design, construction, and commissioning of the expansion project. The team split into several subteams to do the necessary design work, but all designs had to be critiqued and approved by the whole team. Lest we give you a picture of "a match made in heaven," that was *not* the case. The participative management process in this project had some communication problems (some members could participate only on a part-time basis because of shift work), and achieving consensus was difficult. In some situations, the Abilene paradox took over and some significant issues were lost in the process. The Abilene paradox is a concept developed by Jerry B. Harvey in an article published in the summer 1974 issue of *Organization Dynamics*. Harvey states that the inability to manage agreement often causes groups to accept decisions that no group member wants. The paradox is a major problem in most organizations.

What did occur, however, indicates that participative management can lead to greater ownership and commitment by those who get involved. In the design stage, operating people provided a number of ideas that led to more effective designs. Far more ideas were generated by the cross-functionality of the team, thus providing more options from which to choose in design and construction. Many of these ideas were aimed at making the operation of the expansion easier and had to do with standardization in the old plant. On the surface, these improvements may seem insignificant, but in the past they might have been ignored, resulting in some critical operating problems in the plant.

During the construction phase, operators and maintenance technicians "owned" parts of the project. They coordinated the construction and commissioning of projects, made changes with the construction contractors as needed, and even changed design drawings as they saw fit. They stayed with their projects through start-up and assured themselves that the equipment was running smoothly. As a result of their direct involvement, from design to operation, check-outs and start-ups were simpler and smoother than traditionally would have been the case. Bill Cramer, an instrument technician, said, "In the end the start-up went so well that it was just like starting up the old plant when it's shut down for a couple of days." Major systems were built and started up uneventfully, which is almost unheard of in this industry when a traditional approach is used.

Impact of Participative Management

We think some of the ramifications of using participative management are worth noting in this particular case:

1. The original expansion team was instrumental in selecting its leader. The plant manager, Guy Tremblay, invited their participation in the selection process. They established their own criteria for selecting a project leader, considered their options, and provided a short list of three potential candidates for the job. The manager made the final selection from this list.

2. The total instrument and electrical team from the plant's maintenance department was dedicated to the project. What is noteworthy about this fact is that this team was able to be involved in the project while handling all the base maintenance in the old plant with no disruption in service. In fact, when a construction strike occurred, the team completed a $500,000 project that otherwise would have been idled for several weeks and would have resulted in missing critical deadlines.

3. Involving the operating, maintenance, and quality control people in this project allowed the expansion team to handle a much larger workload and with fewer external resources than normally would have been the case. It also allowed people to get into far more detail than they would have traditionally.

4. Sharing construction coordination freed engineers to review details, plan, and allocate work to engineering and construction contractors. Having a field coordinator (previously the

role of the project engineer) was also invaluable and provided opportunities for increased learning.

Organizational Learning

Some of the organizational learnings that resulted from the process that was followed in the Esso PVC case are outlined below:

1. The participative management process identified more potential problems, because more people were committed to the project's success and had input opportunities at all stages.

2. A process should be built in to allow the team to step back and review its mission, goals, and norms. Some significant issues were overlooked as a result of not having the process in place.

3. A great deal of knowledge rested with a few people (the 80–20 rule). This knowledge had to be shared broadly to increase effectiveness.

4. It was difficult to determine who needed to attend which meetings to best utilize the team's resources.

5. It might have been more effective for the subteams to align themselves with whole-shift (operating) teams. This would broaden the direct involvement even more and reduce the pressure on representation to get feedback and input from the teams.

6. For Kevin Gelinas, an operating technician who was part of the expansion team, the greatest eye-opener was that

"Engineers are human just like the rest of us." Nina Pellarin, one of the project's engineers, commented, "Those operators are pretty smart, and easier to work with than I expected." The true lesson underlying their statements is that diverse groups, given a common goal, can work together to achieve something greater than any one group could achieve alone.

The successes of such an endeavor are almost always reduced to a bottom-line question: Did the process result in achieving the goal on time and on budget? The answer in this case is a resounding "Yes!" According to the instrument electrical team, "Our norm was to do it right the first time."

The design and construction stages may have taken more time than required traditionally because of the amount of involvement, but that is to be expected. The shutdown of the old plant and the start-up of the total facility (including the expansion) can best be described as a "nonevent." A large force of Esso Chemical operating, maintenance, and contractor workers was required to achieve this event, but they accomplished it with no injuries and only one minor incident. In this particular industry, that achievement is probably a record! In addition, the project was completed on time and within budget limitations, even with a five-month delay due to slow government approvals and a construction strike that lasted several weeks.

As stated earlier, this project was not a match made in heaven. Although the results were excellent, they could have been better. Many meetings resulted in heated discussions between the various groups of committed stakeholders, and many other problems were encountered. Conflicts were not always handled effectively, and in the end some plant problems were discovered that could have been avoided by the team. However, by applying a participative management approach to this project, the organization learned some valuable lessons about why, when, where, and how to involve people in the business of managing the business. The expansion team clearly would do some things differently if they were doing another project of this type, but every member of the team agreed that this was a far more effective process than any they had encountered in the past.

For us, this case exemplifies what the participative management process can achieve for organizations that are willing to make a clear decision about managing their businesses differently. The choice of participative management as an organizational process is not one that should be taken lightly. It entails a decision to involve people in areas of the business that previously have been the domain of content experts. Once the involvement process begins, people will not be satisfied with low-level involvement; they will demand a bigger slice of the pie. Issues will arise and problems will be uncovered that have, in most organizations, been kept under control. This is due largely to a lack of skill in dealing with such issues, and because of a fear that the problems may be so great that they will result in chaos for the business.

This book shares our combined experiences with participative management and its related issues. We identify and define those issues that organizations "bump into" in their attempts to create participative management, and we illustrate some techniques we have found useful when organizations "step up" to those issues. Participative management is not a perfect system because it involves people and all of their inherent uniqueness as individuals: The presence of two "perfect" people in one room results in an imperfect situation. Participative management's goal is to tap the unique resources of each of those individuals, create a collaborative learning experience, and produce results that are far greater than the sum of the individuals. The benefits far outweigh the risks and problems. The destination for any organization is always worth the cost of the trip—no matter how you measure success.

2

MYTHS OF
PARTICIPATIVE
MANAGEMENT

We open our discussion of participative management with a review of some of the many myths we address any time we use those words—"participative management." As we begin our relationships with clients, we are never facing a blank page. Usually, participative management has been discussed and has risen to at least the vocabulary level of most employees. However, before we can address the issues of participative management, we find it *absolutely necessary* to clarify and demystify the subject. One of the biggest barriers that leaders and change agents face is getting rid of misconceptions that impede the introduction of improved work practices. Although there are many more myths than the ones we have selected, these seem to recur most consistently. What is fascinating to us is the universality of these myths. We find them in government organizations, manufacturing facilities, process facilities (e.g., refineries), hospitals, and small businesses. The pervasive nature of these myths has increased our respect for the power of the misinformation network.

Myths are dangerous in an organization because they usually include half-truths. Myths abound in reference to participative management and teams. For a successful implementation of change in organizational life and behaviors, it is necessary to confront these myths and separate the half-truths from the half-fictions. This confrontation should recognize that mythology is a powerful tool in the hands of those who either want to fight change or impose it. Mythology has its origins in the oral tradition. Stories are passed down and along the communication channels of organizations. Some myths are part of the informal system, whereas others are actually propagated in the formal system. In this chapter, we address both sources of myths, but most importantly we deal with those myths that have now been accepted as part of the formal organizational mindset.

■   **MYTH 1**   ■

Participative Management Can Be Imposed by Top Management

This myth is critical because of the half-truth syndrome. Clearly, participative management is a strategic business decision; therefore, top management has the right and responsibility to make decisions about how the business will be run. This is the half-truth. The half-fiction is that this decision then becomes operational and institutionalized because top management has decided.

As consultants, we see the scenario of key executives who read five chapters of Tom Peters book *In Search of Excellence* and declare that "truth" has been discovered. Because participative management is a business decision, executives confuse its application with other business decisions. If an executive team were to make any one of several business decisions, such as cutting a budget by 10 percent, downsizing across all lines by 15 percent, or selling off a product line, the execution of that decision is immediate and automatic. The executive team moves on to the next agenda item, forgetting the principle identified by Peter Drucker, "Every executive decision can require up to 400 lower level decisions before implementation occurs." However, a business decision involving participative management requires attitudinal and behavioral responses that cannot be executed in immediate and automatic methods. A key step in the process is that senior management must conceptually acknowledge a need to change. However, awareness is only the first step in a long journey to effective process. A more complete road map of the journey is presented in Chapter 3.

The truth side of the half-truth is that, once decided, participative management must be mandated. As a guiding philosophy, it represents a belief and value of how best to do business. You either "talk" or "walk the talk." Credibility is based on consistent behavior, that is, doing the same thing with all people in all situations. Of particular concern with the issue of mandate is the need for being honest about the individual's right to "opt in" or "opt out." A very tough moral dilemma occurs regarding the issue of employees who decide that participation is not for them. This dilemma is a critical test of management's belief in participative management.

The Story of Lydia

A large U.S. organization reorganized its customer service function to a centralized team-based structure. It involved six teams that would be trained together and move from training into a regional customer service team (i.e., the northwest region). A team supervisor was provided until the team became self-managing. At the end of three training sessions, one team member astounded everyone by achieving the highest marks ever seen in the training program. Lydia knew product codes, price lists, stock codes, and details that stood her apart from the others. The training course included seven weeks of technical training and one week of team skills. After two months on the job, Lydia announced, "I do not wish to be a team member. My skills are sufficient enough to operate independently. I will live with all team decisions, so I will not create any problems."

As the manager of the customer service function, Fred had a tough choice. His first approach was to try to get Lydia to change her mind. This produced no results. Lydia was a loner, had high standards, and never worked with others in her life. The moral dilemma was whether Lydia's values and the organizational values could coexist. Needless to say, every other customer service representative was watching this situation with anticipation. Fred did what was necessary: Lydia was given the option of becoming a team member or finding alternative employment. She left.

Many people find this example tough to digest and claim it fundamentally undermines the rights of individuals. However, it was a condition of employment. Lydia knew about teams and accepted the job. Management believed in teams as a business decision and acted accordingly. (More issues concerning the individual are covered in Chapter 5.)

■   **MYTH 2**   ■

Participative Management Is New and Is an Invention or Discovery of the 1980s and 1990s

In an attempt to sell a viewpoint, many people fall into the trap of attacking the past or the status quo. Many so-called gurus describe participative management as an alternative to the autocratic, hierarchical management style of the past. The reality, from our perspective as practicing consultants, is that *effective* organizations have practiced some form of participative management process for years.

What is new is the integration of principles into a coherent strategy, rather than depending on the beliefs and skills of individual managers. Good managers have involved people for years. However, they frequently were required to exercise a guerrilla warfare tactic to protect themselves from the more dominant organizational practices. Participative management is an attempt to legitimize the active involvement of managers, supervisors, and employees in relevant decisions.

Either participative management makes sense or it does not. It is not necessary to attack the self-esteem of the organization's members to justify what is a good business decision. One change management principle states that people resist change if it does not address the issue of protecting their comfort level. Effective managers will fight participative management because it groups them with autocratic managers with whom they cannot and will not relate. Ineffective managers will fight participative management because they risk being asked to make fundamental changes to their way of doing business. There is also an assumed belief that autocratic behavior was always the wrong approach. Where do we, as supporters of participative management, get the right to designate arbitrarily right and wrong? It also assumes that autocratic decisions will have no place in the future process of managing the organization. (This idea of democracy replacing autocracy will be dealt with in Myth 6.)

A Personal Experience

Managers who understood and attempted to apply management by objectives (MBO) were practicing participative management. In 1962, Lorne was privileged to work in a government organization that was managed by an individual who practiced participative management. If anyone asked Tom Foran, "What form of management are you practicing," he would have replied "common sense." His role was to establish goals with the individual, to ensure that we had the skills, resources, and empowerment to be successful and provide support, direction, and feedback as required. Life was simple: Lorne knew what decisions he could and should make, and he knew that Tom was involved in making decisions Lorne never knew about.

As a new employee, it never crossed Lorne's mind that anything unusual was occurring. Thirty years ago, it was comfortable and seemed to be the right way to run a unit. Reality is what happens when that manager leaves and is replaced by a "normal" manager. Tom Foran had already introduced Lorne to the writers of the 1950s and 1960s. They included Kurt Lewin, Rensis Likert, Franz Rothlizberger, Robert Tannenbaum, and Warren Schmidt. The *Harvard Business Review* of that period was filled with articles on a managerial approach that looks suspiciously like participative management.

A search of the writings of the 1950s and 1960s also uncovers Edward Deming, who was preaching his gospel of "quality" to North Americans 30 years ago. While we were philosophically nodding our agreement and simultaneously filing these theories, a very intriguing phenomenon was occurring. Japanese organizations began not only to read these theories, but to institutionalize many of the principles in their workplaces. Deming ultimately moved to Japan, and the Tokyo–San Francisco route of Japan Airlines was used extensively by American management theorists who were essential to the workplace "revolution" occurring in Japan. Many of the social work practices currently found in Japan were the legacy not only of Deming, but also of many other equally farsighted theorists who helped in the integration of quality and statistical control methodologies and worker involvement.

■ **MYTH 3** ■

Participative Management Is for
Wage/Hourly Employees Only

Participative management cannot be delegated. It must be led. In our experience, organizations that fail to understand that managers must model the kind of behaviors they want from employees, also fail to achieve the gains that are possible from the participative process. Managers have a responsibility to their employees that goes beyond simply exhorting them to participate more in the workplace. That responsibility includes helping employees understand how to participate effectively in the organization's business.

Many managers believe that all they have to do is open the valves of participative management and wait for the results to pour in from employees' efforts. Those same managers often find themselves frustrated and disappointed by the lack of results. The lament we hear most frequently from those managers is, "We gave them the training and the freedom to participate, so why aren't they producing?" The most common cause is that managers at all levels are not participating with the employees. Participation extends to *every* employee, from top to bottom, and all must participate together or run the risk of splitting the organization on important business decisions. The biggest payoff from management's participation with employees is never having to overturn a decision made by committed subordinates—a great way to damage the credibility of both the process and the manager. (This issue will be addressed in more detail under Myth 6.)

Participative management does not and should not mean abdication by managers in the decision-making process. What it does mean is that managers actively and consciously join with their employees in the process. The reasons are quite simple: managers have information that their employees do not have, and because managers have a stake in most decisions made within their organizations, their input is necessary to the making of effective decisions. What changes is the nature of their role.

In one organization, a group of employees were asked to redesign their jobs within some fairly fuzzy boundaries. The group did not include a management representative, and did not ask for one. After several months of work, the employees presented their proposal. It was immediately rejected by the managers because it did not represent what they wanted. According to one angry group member, "We met the letter of the mandate, but not the intent. They didn't help us, but they implied that they would accept whatever met the mandate." This unfortunate situation could have been avoided if management had participated in the process with the employees from the beginning. Participation is not a spectator sport; managers at all levels need to lead it by being involved in it.

■   **MYTH 4**   ■

People Want Empowerment, but They Have Been Waiting for Management to Introduce It in the Organization

This myth may be less than a half-truth. It is also a misconception perpetrated by a minority of consultants who have a quick-fix program to sell to managers. These managers either feel a need to improve their organization's bottom-line performance quickly (to become or stay competitive) or they have been told that championing such a program is the new way to get up the organizational ladder.

In our experience, we have not found this to be the case. In fact, just the opposite may be true. Participative management is as much a major change to employees as it is to managers, and change is not welcomed with open arms by most people in existing organizations. It is relatively simple to introduce participative management as the modus operandi in new organizations. Management can design the system up front and make it a condition of employment. Enlightened managers will ensure that participative management is institutionalized. Other managers will lose patience because of their need for control, efficiency, and action, and these managers may succeed in destroying the concept completely. Introducing participative management into an existing organization, which has a history of management by control, is often a lengthy and arduous process. It often requires a rebuilding of trust and a reeducation of the management and the workforce, to say nothing of patience and multiple acts of faith by management before employees believe and buy into the process. Even then, it remains sensitive for a significant length of time, and it can be easily damaged by one management act that violates the concepts of participative management.

Why would employees want participative management when they have been forced to survive most of the management fads of the past three decades? As mentioned in Myth 2, participation in one form or another has been around for years, but it has always been done *to* employees, not *with* them. With each new manager comes a new fad. When one executive introduced his organization's vision of the future centered around participative management, an employee (who would be able to retire in a short time) stood up and told the executive, "We've heard this kind of 'stuff' before. If you're still saying the same thing in two years, then we'll believe that you're serious about making this organization great."

It is unusual to find an existing organization that is setting out to establish participative management as its future management style, with a ready-made critical mass of employees willing to commit to this style. In the initial stages, managers should expect some employees to show a small amount of support, a second group to take a wait-and-see approach, and a third group to actively reject the process as yet another management ploy to increase productivity from an already hard-working workforce. (This myth and the associated issues are further addressed in Chapter 5.)

■   **MYTH 5**   ■

Participative Management Is Organizational Democracy

Democracy, although a noble institution for government, unfortunately is not the goal of participative management. Democracy is characterized by a free election process by which elected representatives are given power for a fixed period to enact policies that the constituency accepts. The cornerstone of democracy is voting and constituency representation. Participative management does not have the same goal or process. It has elements of democracy in the increase of participation and involvement in decisions; however, voting is not necessarily the key tool for resolution. Senior managers are not empowered by a voting constituency, but rather are selected on a judgment of their capability to direct the achievement of the organization's goals and objectives.

There have been some well-documented experiences of industrial democratization in Scandinavia and other parts of Europe. However, these examples consisted of workers selecting representatives to the boards of directors to represent worker interests. We know of no situation where workers' representatives reflect a majority of the board votes. Worker-owned companies, such as TEMBEC in Ontario, are an exception to this principle. This company was saved as an entity from closure by workers who raised capital and took on ownership. Many other examples of this form of democracy exist. However, this is not necessary for an effective participative management process.

Participative management, as a philosophy, emphasizes that workers and managers need to participate in the decision-making processes of the organization. It is essential that the nature of that participation is specified clearly. It does not mean that all organizational decisions will be subjected to review, approval, or sanctioning by employees. Neither does it mean that employees have absolute right and power to make decisions on behalf of the organization or shareholders. The key to participative management lies in specifying three types of organizational decisions and clarifying everyone's responsibility for each type (these types are discussed further in Chapter 5):

1. *Independent decisions.* These decisions are made by managers/supervisors/individuals based on:

- Clear responsibility allocation for that decision
- Organizational acceptance of that authority to make that type of decision
- A full information base to permit effective decision making.

These decisions are the lubrication of the decision-making process. They represent the many day-to-day issues that do not require team discussion, input, or agreement. These decisions are accepted by everyone, and the individual making them does not need to expect challenges.

2. *Collaborative decisions.* These decisions are made by a manager or group of individuals that has been given the responsibility and authority to decide on this issue. However, these decisions cannot be imposed without input, participation, and advice from those people who will be affected by it. It would be unwise for the decision maker not to seek help, guidance, and ideas. Asking for help does not mean that the decision maker is forced to agree with it or accept the options provided by others. By asking for input, a person has not given up the *right* to make the final decision.

In this type, the manager asks for recommendations and as such can overturn a team's proposal. This is probably the most contentious area of participative management. In countless instances, we have seen steering committees, managers, or management teams reject proposals from teams, individuals, or task forces. This does not mean a rejection of participative management; it means that unclear expectations were provided to teams that began to believe they were decision makers, not simply recommenders. Participative management believes that better decisions will be made because of the participation of the right people in the decision process. It does not extend to include all those people in the final approval process on all issues. Management is always accountable to the shareholders. Employees are not. If the nature of the decision involves shareholder protection, management cannot delegate that responsibility to employees.

3. *Team/individual-empowered decisions.* These decisions are made by the team or an empowered individual and do not

require approval or review by management or steering committees. In these types of decisions, full responsibility is vested in a person or a team that is informed enough, mature enough, skilled enough, and caring enough to decide on the best course of action. Management has the responsibility to provide boundaries to ensure that these decisions will be successful. The decisions are not subject to veto, so management must ensure the team is successful. Two elements are required for success:

- Information is provided to ensure that all issues are addressed.
- Boundaries are in place that allow discretion but ensure success.

Team decisions will be limited to those issues that affect team actions and results. The world of participative management is not a world of team decisions. It is managers/individuals deciding when that is appropriate and managers and teams working together to enable managers to make the best overall decisions and to permit teams to decide about those issues that are their responsibility.

■   **MYTH 6**   ■

Participative Management Means Teams and Leads to Self-Directing Teams

Many organizations in both the private and service sectors have developed successful participative management approaches that did not include teams because they simply did not make sense. If no *interdependence* exists between workers, why would you force them into teams? The only plausible answer we can find is that teams are the way things are done today. So are mergers and acquisitions, but they do not seem to work very well if you look at their track record, and not everyone is getting into that game. Let us be clear: We are 100 percent for teams and teamwork— where it makes sense as a structural intervention under the participative management umbrella. The problem is that too many managers, in introducing participative management into their organizations, leap to the conclusion (without much forethought) that teams are a natural ingredient for success. How the organization and the work are structured, in terms of potential negative or positive impact on participative management, is a critical element in planning for implementation of the process. We caution managers against the irresistible urge to force fit the structure and the work into the process. The plan, if you have one, has to make sense to those who will live and work within the system. If you do opt for teams, leave room for individuals to participate in the participative management process. Individuals are the building blocks of teams and organizations, and we do not feel that they should always make the sacrifice for the sake of the team. Teams are not infallible entities.

A Story of an Unnatural Team

A client of ours has decided that empowerment is dependent on a cohesive shift team. This means people are scheduled to work together on an ongoing basis. Because the shift people run the unit, this makes a lot of sense. However, the shift team has been expanded to include maintenance mechanics. Traditionally, these people have worked days and are called in on overtime to repair critical equipment. The client wants the mechanics to work shifts so the team can be fully independent. The negative factors are:

- There is not enough work to justify twenty-four hour coverage.
- The salary cost of doubling the maintenance team is unprofitable.

As one mechanic so aptly said, "Now mechanics can go in at night and sleep with operators who don't have enough to do." This is a classic example of not requiring a team.

Self-Directing Teams

Self-directing teams are included in this myth, and frankly we believe the jury is still out on the issue. First, we are concerned about the overuse of terminology such as "leaderless teams." This term implies no structure, no boundaries, and no rules—everything is up for grabs. It is doubtful that many organizations can survive, let alone succeed, under these conditions. According to one worker, "Leaderless teams are no big deal. Based on the quality of leadership we've seen . . . we've been leaderless for three years now."

Second, the evidence about self-directing teams and their ability to operate successfully appears to be inconclusive. In one petrochemical plant we have been associated with, the goal was to eliminate supervision altogether and have self-directing teams manage their own affairs. Because this organization was new, the goal seemed attainable—theoretically. Within two years of start-up, each team had two supervisors. The reasons were simple enough: The teams of 21 people were too large for one person to supervise. A high number of team members felt ignored by supervision. The complex was so large geographically that the "team" was actually two natural teams when operating the equipment. The single supervisor simply could not provide the necessary support for the team to operate the equipment effectively. We are not saying that self-directing teams cannot succeed if they are given the appropriate resources in terms of skill-building, knowledge, information, and facilitation resources. Our experience indicates, however, that more organizations are moving away from this concept because of the numerous problems they have encountered.

Self-directing teams may indeed evolve from the participative management process as those teams grow in skill maturity, but we do not feel they are necessarily a goal in participative management. (We discuss these issues in more detail in Chapter 4.)

■   **MYTH 7**   ■

Participative Management Is Free

Participative management is not free, but it also cannot be bought. The organization has to create an environment that will allow people to accept the belief that participative management has a real payoff for the organization and the employees. This has a significant cost attached to it since the organization probably will have to ensure that everyone understands the new values, attitudes, and culture necessary for participative management's success. What is the budget for implementing this critical strategy? Is there one? Nobody builds a plant or office building without a budget, so why would anyone plan to redesign an organization without a cost–benefit analysis and a budget to support the plan?

Here are some facts to think about. In one chemical plant with a population of about 600 employees, the reeducation and buy-in process took about two years at a cost of approximately three million dollars. That process included visits by groups of 6 to 12 people from the plant to many organizations across North America with successful participative management systems in place. It also included the training of most employees in a variety of skill areas related to participative management. Their training and development budget went from 2 percent of salary and benefit costs to about 20 percent, representing a significant shift in priorities. The result was not a 100-percent buy-in of all employees, but the creation of a very significant critical mass and a much higher probability of success for participative management as the way for all employees to do business together in the future. It also clarified the issues to be resolved, new procedures for addressing those issues, and more importantly, a willingness to explore new alternatives for resolving those issues in a win–win fashion.

This type of example indicates to us that participative management is a cost-effective strategy, but is definitely not free. It requires a heavy commitment of time and resources. If an organization must err, it should err on the high side because many unpredictable costs can be associated with "getting there."

■   **MYTH 8**   ■

Consensus Is the Only Way to Make Decisions in a Participative Environment

This is known as the "paralytic myth." If a team decides that the *only* method of resolving situations is through consensus, they have doomed themselves to a time frame that may cause many team members to lose interest. Consensus is, and should be, an important tool for achieving commitment. However, it is not the only tool. Furthermore, consensus must not be confused with unanimity. Team members regularly confuse consensus with a need to have everyone agree. As process consultants, we frequently see team members polarize because of a disagreement over certain proposals or issues. This usually is followed by a lengthy discussion attempting to get individuals to change their minds and agree with the majority.

Definition of Consensus

Consensus is a result of a discussion between team members that reflects a *willingness* to actively support the group's decision. It does not necessarily mean all members are in agreement. It means the disagreement is *not* sufficiently rooted that any member will *not* try to make the decision work. Consensus should be limited to those situations in which it is imperative that team members actively support the decision.

Consensus should also be restricted to those issues that are within the empowerment of the team, that is decisions that will be implemented directly by the team without management review. If a steering committee recommends proposals for review and approval by a third party, then consensus seems too elaborate a process. A majority vote or a recommendation of a range of options reflecting the different viewpoints would probably suffice.

An old expression says, "If you give a person a hammer . . . everything begins to look like a nail." Teams need to recognize that a range of decision-making alternatives exists for different situations. Some typical examples are:

- *Consensus*
  - What is it?
    - — A total commitment to the group decision, whether or not the minority agrees with the result.
  - When to use it:
    - — Commitment to the solution is critical to successful implementation.
    - — "Whether to" decisions are the subject.
    - — There are no further opportunities to readdress this issue.
  - Examples:
    - — Work design.
    - — Changes to reward system.
    - — Choice of leader/team member.
    - — Choice of group process.
- *Majority Vote*
  - What is it?
    - — Fifty percent + one.
    - — An agreement to go along with the majority, but not necessarily willing to support the result.
  - When to use it:
    - — Minor issues do not need 100 percent support.
    - — Huge populations are involved and there is no forum for resolving minority positions.
  - Examples:
    - — Agreement to shift schedules for a new plant prior to start-up.
    - — Choice of rotating chairperson/scribe/facilitator in team.

- *Unanimity*
  - What is it?
    - — Unanimity involves gaining 100 percent agreement, not simply willingness to go along with the group.
  - When to use it:
    - — Emotional issues create an insurmountable barrier to consensus.
    - — Responsibility for the decision significantly impacts each player.
  - Examples:
    - — Agreement to team/organization values.
    - — Establishment of team goal statements.
- *Imposition*
  - What is it?
    - — A *mandated* solution directed by someone with the authority to impose such a solution.
  - When to use it:
    - — The issue is truly non-negotiable in terms of responsibility.
    - — The group will not accept responsibility for the solution.
    - — Low-impact/short-term solutions are needed.
  - Examples:
    - — An empowered team leader decides on location for team meetings.
    - — The clarification and delivery of boundaries or non-negotiables for a team task.
- *Plop*
  - What is it?
    - — A suggestion that gets accepted without any discussion.

- When to use it:
  - — A group has no formal agenda, leader, or process.
  - — The group is hopelessly stalled and seeks redirection.
  - — The issue/solution has been prearranged.
- Examples:
  - — "Why don't we all describe our version of the problem. My problem is _____."

As an illustration of the overuse of consensus, one particular client group had a 30 million dollar expansion project for an existing manufacturing operation. Early during deliberations, the group agreed consensus would be the only tool for agreement. Team meetings averaged eight to ten hours at a stretch and involved thirty people who represented management, engineering, operators, maintenance, and lab personnel. Specialized groups were formed to focus on specific subcomponents of the overall design. They were given no empowerment to make decisions on their specialty. Every issue had to be presented to the whole team and consensus reached before progress could be made. The result was "paralysis by analysis and consensus." People with no technical knowledge were given the same power of approval and review as those who actually understood the difference between 1/4-inch and 1/8-inch piping. The team was three months behind schedule.

The project team reviewed its self-imposed handicap of consensus, and the team got back on schedule. Effective decisions began to occur. Consensus was restricted to those issues on which it was necessary that the whole team support the decision. By the end of the project, the team was two months ahead of schedule and 10 percent under budget.

■ **MYTH 9** ■

Participative Management Is a Program, Not a Process

People in organizations have been subjected to so many different training panaceas that there should be no surprise that they see participative management as another "flavor of the month." Every time the organization launches the next "key to success" program, the disillusionment increases. One client has successfully initiated MBO, Synectics, Kepner Tregoe, Innovation in the '80s, Quality of Work Life, and Behavior Modeling from the human resources division. Other "salvations" have probably been omitted inadvertently from the above litany.

What makes participative management different is that it *is not* and *should not* be driven by the human resource department. It is a business decision, not a human resources decision. Human resources has a role in supporting the process, but not in leading it. Second, it is not a course. Although there is a definite need to include skill development as part of the process, it is more important to recognize the limitations of training as the main vehicle for participative management. An appropriate phrase of unknown origin, but which we wish we had said, is, "You cannot train your way out of something you managed your way into."

Participative management must have at least a three-year plan that clearly identifies a transference of authority, accountability, access to necessary information, and skills to those people who will make the operating decisions of the future. Participative management is about changing structures, reward systems, procedures, and relationships. The changes cannot be successfully introduced if there is any intention of later with-drawal or replacement by another "flavor of the month."

Table 2.1 compares typical management training programs with a participative management process.

TABLE 2.1

Management Program	Participative Management Process
Timing • Fixed (e.g., 3 days/5 days)	*Timing* • Open-ended with a range of interventions (e.g., 3 to 5 years)
Focus • Skills/attitude • Individual	*Focus* • Organization results
Timing of Process • Short term	*Timing of Process* • Long term
Results • Motivation • External • Remains with a champion forever • Short-term success	*Results* • Ongoing behavior • Structures • Relationships • System wide • Internalized by every employee
Responsibility • Human resources • Training strategy this year	*Responsibility* • All managers and individuals • Business strategy for 3 to 5 years
Priority • When we have time • When times are good	*Priority* • The way we live
Services • Single guru and consultants to support	*Services* • Many sources (i.e., not guru driven) • Other organizations • Other practitioners/workers/ managers
Method • One right way • Top–down	*Method* • No right way • Everybody

■   **MYTH 10**   ■

Participative Management Leads to Error-Free Quality Performance

This is an extremely tricky myth. The half-truth is that partici-pative management leads to quality performance. The half-fiction is that it provides error-free performance. There is no doubt that empowerment and involvement lead to higher quality decisions and performance. The bottom-line results of plants that have moved to participative management prove the payoff. Tridon Manufacturing in Oakville, Ontario, went from a $3 mil-lion loss to a $1.3 million profit in two years. Bausch and Lomb in Texas created a parallel unit for people who opted out of partici-pative management. Within two years, the parallel unit was shut down as unprofitable. A similar unit on the same site provided a healthy return on investment under a participative management philosophy.

The fascinating half-fiction is the concept of error-free performance. The fascination lies in two dimensions:

1. Errors are part of a traditional form of management, and the participative management philosophy should not ex-pect to be without them.

2. Failure is the fuel of growth. Not only should failure be expected, but it should be encouraged. The lack of failure represents the lack of risk taking and experimentation.

A key concern of participative management is how failure is managed. The traditional approach involves extremely un-healthy responses to failure, such as:

- Finger pointing
- Defensiveness
- Denial
- Covering up
- Protecting vital parts of the anatomy
- Justifying the inevitability of failure.

In participative management, failure is programmed as a learning experience to be shared so it is not repeated. Paul Cook, the chairman of Raychem, is probably one of the most positive managers of failure in the United States. He defines "failure as learning" and the "failure to learn" from failure as poor management." To Cook, failure is part of the cost of doing business.

Failure that is not shared is failure that is doomed for repetition. That repetition is unacceptable because it is unnecessary. A major U.S. client introduced a column entitled "Failure of the Month" in the corporate newsletter. The purpose was to legitimize failure and permit people to openly discuss the learning that occurred. Every vice-president was ordered to contribute one column. To not have erred was to not have pushed the limits of the business. The column title has since been tempered to "The Learning of the Month"; however, the point has been made.

HOW TO MANAGE FAILURE

Learning how to *manage failure* is synonymous with learning how to *manage growth*. In participative management, this is one of the most difficult skills required of a manager. In a society that worships winners, we have low tolerance for the losses that lead to winning. We glorify Edison's achievements and forget his words. When asked about the 2,000 failed experiments that led to the discovery of tungsten as the appropriate filament for light bulbs, he said, "I have eliminated 2,000 possibilities that narrows the field for success." In modern organizations, he might have been fired for excessive failure.

Several common-sense principles can help managers convert failure to learning. These are discussed in the following sections.

Principle 1: Managing the Tolerance of Failure

This is a fairly simple yet difficult issue. Imagine an employee bringing a proposal to you to change something. In your wisdom, the proposed solution is 90 percent of what you consider to be the optimal solution. What do you do?

The traditional response is, "That's a great idea. Let's talk about several things that are missing. If you did X and Y, we can turn this into an excellent idea." This response removes ownership from the originator and transfers, ownership to the manager. It is no longer your employee's idea. It is yours. The maximum expected commitment from the employee is 50 percent.

The participative management response, however, is, "Go for it. Let me know when you need help. I think you have a great idea that will improve the business." This response ensures that 100 percent of the commitment to make it work remains with the originator of the idea. The 10 percent of "perfection" you give away is your "tolerance for failure." It is critical to understand the mythical 100 percent. That's the way the manager would do it.

If the percentage of success was 60 percent, then obviously some involvement becomes necessary, but what is equally necessary is understanding the required tolerance for failure.

Principle 2: *Managing the Arena of Failure*

Failure is often dreaded because it is seen as absolute. In reality, failure is rarely absolute. Certain arenas of an individual's job are absolutely error proof. Bigger areas, however, provide an arena of discretionary failure. Unfortunately the employee rarely knows which is which. The manager's job is to clearly define the arena of discretion and the arena of discretionary failure. This is known as *managing* the arena of failure. Perhaps it should be known as *communicating* the arena of failure. This concept is diagrammatically represented in Figure 2.1.

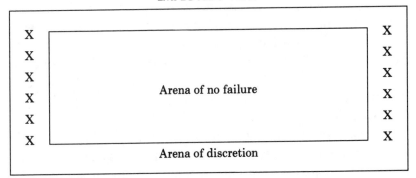

FIGURE 2.1 VIEWS OF ARENA OF FAILURE

In Figure 2.1 the arena of no failure represents those parts of the job that must be performed 100 percent error free. They might include safety, legality, quality, or values activities. The arena of discretionary failure indicates those parts of the job on which failure is not fatal. It is in these arenas that managers *could* and *should* encourage the growth of individuals. The size of the arena of discretion differs from employee to employee. A "rookie" probably operates with a small arena of discretionary activity, whereas a "veteran" has much greater scope for exercising empowered behavior.

Principle 3: Create a Failure Balance Sheet

Some failure is inevitable. It usually represents a single error in a chain of successful behaviors. What stifles people's growth is the tendency to ignore forty examples of success and focus on the single event of failure. This syndrome is reflected in the parent's saying to a child, "I don't care about your six A's. What about this C?"

The hotel industry continually tries to isolate positive performance to ensure that the credit side of the behavioral balance sheet is covered. At a recent guest appreciation night at the Holiday Inn in Sarnia, Ontario, Lorne was sought out to identify an example of effective customer service. The manager of the hotel has a discretionary fund to reward specific examples of pcsitive performance. The creation of a credit side for performance enhances our ability to deal less emotionally with the negative side.

Behavioral balance sheets not only are useful for managers, but are important for employees. There is a rumor circulating that "managers are human too." A manager who firmly believes in empowerment will, from time to time, make a decision in violation of his or her beliefs and values. Under pressure, the manager might unilaterally make a decision that is more properly the responsibility of an individual or team. What happens frequently is unfair. After months of seeing positive team-based behaviors, the team reacts by saying, "See, I told you they didn't believe in participative management." In these instances, not only is confession good for the soul, but it is good for rebuilding relationships. Instead of defending his or her "right" to make decisions, the manager should admit to the team, "I made a mistake. Let's talk about it and learn from it. What can I do to keep it from happening again?"

Empowerment of individuals/teams includes the potential for errors. It is not necessarily more dangerous than letting managers make all the decisions. Therefore, to be successful, empowerment must mean the creation of a failure management policy. People will walk a very high tightrope if they believe a safety net is in place. People will not accept empowerment without the failure safety net.

SUMMARY

Leaders who decide to radically change the historical methods of doing business take on a challenge of great difficulty. The challenge is increased when misconceptions and myths are allowed to complicate the picture. We have attempted to clarify what participative management is about by attacking some of the commonly held myths that "fuzzify" a fairly straight-forward philosophy. Table 2.2 summarizes the main issues discussed in this chapter.

MYTHS OF PARTICIPATIVE MANAGEMENT

TABLE 2.2

Participative Management Is	*Participative Management Is* Not
• Done "with" people	• Done "to" people
• A business-based decision/strategy	• Human resources department–based decision
• Empowering teams and individuals to make decisions that relate to their own work	• Having *all* decisions made by individuals/teams
• Increasing empowerment for the *whole* organization	• Empowering a select few
• A process that requires ongoing leadership and change in behavior from the top	• Imposed on an organization without active leadership
• A planned process of change	• An unplanned journey
• "Walking the talk," that is, doing what you say	• Talking a philosophy but taking no action
• Getting into the ring	• Talking a good fight
• A consolidation of many different and practical insights about people and work	• A brilliant discovery of the Japanese
• Redesigning the way all work gets done	• Redesigning the job of the hourly worker
• Tapping the potential of the people	• Reacting to a revolution of social values
• Clearly assigned responsibilities for the future	• Anarchy
• Teams and individuals participating collaboratively	• *Only* about "self-directed teams"
• The effective utilization of people	• *Only* about downsizing
• Expensive to introduce, with potential high returns	• Free
• Making effective decisions	• *Only* about consensus
• A long-term process	• A program with a finite beginning and end
• About developing organizations into "learning systems"	• Eliminating failure

3

ISSUES FOR THE ORGANIZATION

Undertaking participative management has a traumatic impact on the organization, its work units, individual managers, supervisors, and employees. This chapter focuses on the key issues that need to be addressed by senior management if participative management is to yield significant benefits. Although our focus is on senior management, the issues discussed are vital for internal and external consultants who advise or assist in the implementation of participative management.

We do not believe the issues we have chosen represent a complete agenda of participative management. Anyone who has experienced an attempt to implement participative management will question why we did not include other issues. We chose to include:

1. Issues we have personally experienced as the most significant. Others may feel differently about our choices because of their own experiences.

2. Issues that represent both good examples and failures. Because participative management is working, a focus on the negative is not necessarily the best and only learning vehicle.

We did not intend that every word in this book appeal to everyone. We expect readers to be somewhere in the process of participative management, whether they are considering the process, are working toward full implementation, or are looking for a fine-tuning improvement of an already operating process. Thus, we have organized this chapter in terms of issues. Each section focuses on different organizational issues and can be read and applied independently, as needs require.

A CASE FOR PARTICIPATIVE MANAGEMENT

Serendipity is the fortunate situation when two events accidently come together to create an opportunity. Such an event happened the week before the first draft of this book. At a year-end review meeting with a client in the petrochemical industry, a challenge was presented that dovetailed into the contents of this book. We hope it provides a practical example of what participative management means, how to get it started, and how to sustain it through to success. The following description uses fictitious names for an actual situation in a client company.

Jim Doe was the newly appointed plant manager for World Chemicals. Jim had been a client for several smaller management consultations while he was the engineering manager for the site. We were briefing Jim, in his new position, and his human resource manager on the status of work performed across the site. Much of this work, initiated by Jim's predecessor, had been directed at specific skill development and change management in the organization. It represented a series of useful but scattered approaches to increasing teamwork and productivity.

The organization itself was suffering from an intense "identity crisis." Several months earlier, the plant operation, now run by Jim, was sold to a new owner. This was less than three years since the plant's previous change in ownership. Thus, there had been three owners in three years. The good news was that the new owners were interested specifically in this product-line business and had plans for its future. The former owner, who had purchased the entire complex for control of a specific feedstock source, viewed some of the other product business as merely part of the package. Jim felt that the uncertainty that came with the new ownership created opportunity. Rather than letting this identity crisis paralyze the organization, Jim saw a chance to forge ahead and create a new environment.

Jim had come into his job with a vision and a belief about where he wanted the organization to go. He saw an organization that was restructured to functional teams and drafted a position paper on integrated teams. He saw a business being run on the basis of participation and empowerment of decision making at the most appropriate level. But he also saw teams that had to integrate with each other. He was concerned about introducing a concept of "team fiefdom." Fiefdoms occur when individual teams stake out their own boundaries and fail to consider the organization as a whole. It is an old French word that describes the tendency of Scottish clans to fight among themselves for no apparent reason except history, boredom, and physical exercise. He drew an organizational chart that was turned upside down. His position was on the bottom of the chart, and the teams that produced the "product" were on the top. It was clear that the role of the "lower levels" was to support the only people in the organization who made the product—the workers.

Then Jim began to fill his key team leader positions. The restructuring provided an opportunity to select those people Jim felt could and would support the achievement of his vision. The appointments made by Jim were restricted to his own team members. He felt that selection for other teams should be made by the appropriate team leaders. Of particular interest was the statement Jim included in the list of first announcements:

> Some may be surprised by the individuals chosen by me to be part of my management team. A key criteria that I used for selection was leadership ability. In a petrochemical complex we assume technical competence is essential for safety and environmental reasons, but it should not be the main criteria for promotion.

By this point, Jim had circulated his vision, and restructured and appointed his management team. His question for the consultant was, "How do I accomplish my vision?" A vision without a plan is like a political leader without any votes. It presents an excellent opportunity to philosophize, but nothing happens. The following sections of this chapter, and we hope the other chapters, attempt to provide Jim (and others) with some direction and focus.

■   ISSUE 1   ■

Need for a Road Map

After much thought, you have decided to implement participative management in your business as a major strategy for improving organizational performance and industry competitiveness. You want to become the best in the marketplace, and you've given some thought to how you might introduce participative management to your subordinate managers and how you might deal with their reactions. You also have given some thought to how employees might react to the introduction of such a process into the workplace. You've also had passing thoughts about how existing people systems might affect the effective implementation of the participative management process, but that's really the responsibility of the human resources department . . . or is it? To implement participative management successfully and to reap the considerable rewards that are possible when you get it institutionalized, you need to get past the thinking stage and devise a road map or plan.

Why a Plan Is Important

As we pointed out at the beginning of this chapter, participative management will have a traumatic effect on each organization. It affects every person at every level, and usually requires major changes to existing structures and systems. Because it has such wide-ranging impact, it needs to be carefully planned if management intends to create a high-performing, competitive organization for the future. We are not talking about a rigid plan that must be adhered to blindly. We are suggesting a plan that encompasses some critical components, and provides people in the organization with a sense that management has a plan for proceeding on the journey.

How to Address the Issue

We believe the road map should be capable of answering these frequently asked questions:

- Why is change necessary?
- What is the change to be?
- Who is involved in the change?
- How is the change to be made?
- When does this change start?

Why Is Change Necessary?

This question elicits different responses from managers depending on market share, overall performance, competitiveness within the industry, and a host of other factors that you as a manager probably know better than we do. Whatever your reasons are, they need to be clear and credible to employees. They must make sense if you expect people to commit their personal resources of time and energy to the goals of participative management and the success of the business.

In understanding the need for change, it is important to remember that change is driven by need. People will *not* accept change if the driving forces for change are not relevant to them. The TOPS model provides a tool for understanding these forces. The model is meant to provide a means of assessing the rationale for change and can be used to communicate the necessity for upsetting the status quo. It states that change has to be created by a need. Change for the sake of change is an orphan. Those affected by a change will question the reasons why the change was introduced. Four dominant needs justify change:

T = Threat

O = Opportunity

P = Problems

S = Success.

These needs are discussed in the following sections.

Threat   A change will be perceived as necessary if there is significant *fear* for the future. Fear is a motivator for change. In the case of Jim and his leadership team, several threats were behind their decision to change the operating philosophy of the business:

- Increased competition from global competitors would eventually erode the company's client base.

- North American free trade exposed the company's current market share to duty-free competition.
- Twenty-year-old technology would create a greater threat of environmental problems and make it more difficult to meet the higher quality standards required in the marketplace.

The conclusion was obvious. If the team did nothing to address these threats the operation would probably not survive.

Opportunity Another driving force is greed. This is not negative greed, but an acceptance of the validity of people asking, "What's in it for me?" Just as fear creates an acceptance for change, so does opportunity. People will be motivated to change if they can identify sufficient payoffs for the effort involved. Some opportunities appeared to Jim and his team:

- Empowerment of teams could give managers more time to address the longer term issues, such as product development, environmental protection, and planned maintenance.
- A significant reduction of "off-spec" production would result from the assumption of ownership at the workplace.
- The team concept would allow for less need to provide specialized support services, thereby increasing the flexibility of the work force.
- Job satisfaction would increase for the individual in the organization. Teams would provide a chance for employees to make a contribution and to feel that work is not merely a place to show up and perform repetitive tasks forever.

Problems If problems cause enough trouble, people will entertain the thought of change. If an operating problem continues to occur despite attempts to fix it, then some form of new response must be considered. In justifying change, some form of problem must be resolved. In Jim's case, the following problems existed:

- Maintenance costs were increasing because of the age of the equipment.
- Environmental controls were increasing, and technology alone would not solve the problem.
- The workforce—both management and hourly employees— were still suffering from an identity crisis as a result of the several ownership changes.

Success   Although envy is one of the seven deadly sins, it is also a motivating factor for many people. It is natural to make comparisons among different organizations. If people see a competitor who can outproduce them, make better quality products, and outperform their financial results, it seems reasonable to consider learning how to be like them.

In Jim's situation, this was a major driving force. The plant is part of a multinational company, and several other plants produced similar products. A Texas plant had a better safety record, a better return on investment, and a significantly easier time getting additional funding for expansion and improvement. A logical question became, "Why can't we perform like them?" Teams were part of the answer.

What Is the Change to Be?

This question can best be answered by a vision statement. "Vision" is the new management buzzword for the 1990s; however, if you ask a group of managers or consultants to define the term, you will get a variety of responses. It is important to define what you mean when you use the term in your own organization. We think of vision as defining what the organization will look like, or need to look like, at some given point in the future—say 5 to 10 years—after participative management has been implemented successfully. Here are two techniques we have used to help managers develop visions for their organizations:

1. Ask yourself what the organization would be like if everything was exactly as you would like it to be. What would be happening? What values would be evident? What would people be doing? Avoid being too specific. A vision is a word painting of the desired end state, a description of an organization at a state of realized potential.

2. Imagine that it is five years in the future (or whatever number of years you choose for the change to participative management to occur) and you have achieved your vision. You have invited a group of your best customers to join you for a helicopter tour over your organization to allow them to see how it works. How would they describe what they saw during the tour?

There are other techniques to help managers with the visioning process. What is important is to create a statement that lets others visualize the end state as clearly as you do. See Appendix I for further examples and a discussion of vision statements.

Who Is Involved in the Change?

This answer should be obvious. Participative management is for everyone in the organization because they all have something of value to contribute, and they all are stakeholders in the outcome. Some organizations even take the position that participation is optional until it becomes mandatory. This is a hard-line approach to what many people call "soft stuff," but it may be necessary if survival is the prize.

Perception is a major concern on this issue. Rampant cynicism exists in the workplace. People often have been told for so long that a company may not survive that they no longer believe it. Two conflicting principles cause this to happen:

1. *Principle of invincibility.* Employees convince themselves that the organization can fight off any form of attack: "After all," they may rationalize, "the company survived the recession of 1980 to 1982, didn't it?"

2. *Principle of insignificance.* As employees of a small plant in a multibillion dollar company, people do not think they represent a significant threat to the parent company. For instance, they may think, "Exxon would not bother with a little chemical plant in Sarnia" or "General Electric is too big to worry about a small plant in New York State." If survival is the issue, you need to be prepared to prove it or to be ignored.

How Is the Change to Be Made?

Making the change to participative management means defining long- and short-term goals, as well as the action steps required to achieve those goals. We suggest target dates because people need to stay focused during the transition from where the organization is today, to where it intends to be when it attains each goal along the path to the vision. We recommend flexibility in the target dates, largely because change rarely occurs as planned, and detours and delays often occur along the way. Furthermore, organizations usually find they missed something in the planning for implementation of participative management. This is not an engineering task; it is a human task. Although it is difficult to obtain predictability and stability during the change process, it is a challenge that must be undertaken to institutionalize and internalize the process.

The plan also should outline how and in what areas employees at different levels will be involved in the change process. They have a need to know as much as you can tell them about their involvement. However, managers need to be careful that they do not take this step too far, or they will find themselves in a control mode again—the very thing they are trying to move away from with participative management. The most important point employees need to understand is that management does not know all the answers about participative management. As the organization gains in experience with the process, course corrections may be necessary to the initial plan. When those corrections become decision points, they should be made in a consultative manner with input from those affected. As organizations move deeper into the change, the plan for moving forward should evolve and become clearer and more specific.

When Does this Change Start?

The answer is, "Now!" Once you announce the change to participative management, you must take action immediately as evidence that management is sincere and serious. Your first actions are crucial in that they set the tone for the whole process, so select carefully. Your credibility, and that of the participative management process, will hinge on initial actions and decisions. One such action might be for the manager with the vision to meet with small groups of employees and have frank discussions with them to explore their reactions to, and concerns about, participative management as an organizational process. The manager probably will not enjoy all these sessions—remember the myth about everyone wanting participative management—but there are almost always some pleasant surprises for the manager in terms of early wins (if he or she truly is sincere) in the form of support for participative management from unexpected sources.

We think a couple of points are noteworthy. The presentation of a manager's vision and the road map for achieving participative management do not require the manager to have the presentation skills of an evangelist or the style of a Tom Peters to gain support. It requires honesty and candor about the five questions discussed above and a visible willingness to commit the resources needed to make participative management an integral part of the organization's culture. Managers do not need to rush out and enroll in a Dale Carnegie course. Employees will know if a manager is serious and will commit to trying new ways if a manager is viewed as credible and if there is acceptance of the need to change.

Role of Employee Representatives

A good strategy for gaining support quickly is to involve employee representatives early in the process. The planning stage is an excellent place to start, particularly if you have a union or another form of employee bargaining group. This involvement provides an early opportunity to test your vision and find out where and why participative management may encounter the greatest resistance in your organization. You can then plan proactively for its reduction or elimination. If managers gain the support of employee representatives, elected by their peers because of their commitment to employee well-being, then the implementation process will go more smoothly because both groups share a common goal in participative management. We are not stating categorically that this strategy always produces positive results. Indeed, we know of situations where the results of this well-intended decision were disastrous, but these are the exceptions and not the norm. We believe the sooner management involves the informal leaders of employee groups in the whole process, the more likely it is that participative management will succeed.

The most successful examples of early participation by employee representatives that we see are those where the manager invites the representatives, or their leaders, to serve on an organizational steering committee that guides the change effort. The steering committee usually includes the top manager and people who report directly to him or her. Using a team approach with the employee representatives makes great sense as it allows regular testing and challenging of participative management concepts and values. It ensures a continual flow of information into and out of the steering committee, keeping the feedback process open, and it reduces the need to recycle issues and decisions. Furthermore, it is an excellent way to monitor the pulse of the organization, which can be invaluable in the change process. There are other positive by-products of this strategy, not the least of which is the improvement in relationships between managers and employee representatives. Both groups gain a new understanding of each other and usually find through interactions that they have more in common than they realized. We strongly endorse the idea of building employee representatives into your plan, as it can only help the participative management process in the long run.

Managers should avoid perceiving resistance to participative management as a personal attack on them. It is normal and inevitable, and it can be overcome. This type of change requires tenacity and a firm belief that the organization can achieve the leader's vision through the actions of all its employees. There are examples of participative management in every industry around the world today; no manager should feel that he or she is alone in this endeavor.

Force-Field Analysis

A technique that managers have found useful in determining what they need to include in their participative management plan is Kurt Lewin's force-field analysis. It is a simple but powerful technique for identifying and evaluating the strength of forces within the organization that may help or hinder the organization's efforts to change to the participative management process (see Figure 3.1). Once these forces are identified, plans can be developed for reducing or eliminating hindering forces and for strengthening helping forces. The goal is to create a participative culture in which all employees feel involved and empowered. Although many other techniques may be as effective, this has been the most successful for us in our work with managers.

We have had the most success when we weigh each of the forces listed in Figure 3.1, using a seven-point scale with the following weights as guidelines:

1—Worth mentioning, but minimal effect on situation.

4—Some effect on situation.

HELPING FORCES		*HINDERING FORCES*
• Union executive involvement/ support for change	**S** **T** **A** **T** **U** **S** **Q** **U** **O**	• Union agreements/contracts
• Leader credibility is high		• Some managers against change
• Some head office executive support		• Existing reward system
• Success of other companies in our industry		• Lack of corporate support
• Could create more opportunities for development/advancement		• Viewed as latest fad
• Better working conditions/ relationships		• Professionals view it as "for hourly employees only," feel that they will lose power
• Better returns on bottom line		• Lack of specifics about end results

FIGURE 3.1   FORCE-FIELD ANALYSIS

7—Critical factor in terms of its effect on situation. May need external help to resolve.

Weighting provides a fairly accurate picture of the current situation, and indicates where to focus valuable resources. Over the years, we have found that in some organizations, it is most effective to first address forces with a weighting of 4 or 5. This allows some early successes and builds energy for tackling those weighted 7. Success is easy to build on, but failure leaves you with nothing.

The natural tendency of organizations is to conclude that they should strengthen the helping forces immediately. When this approach is taken, it frequently gives rise to new hindering forces, or strengthens existing ones. The result usually is no change in the status quo. We suggest instead that organizations address ways to reduce or eliminate the hindering forces. This is often most effective because it allows the driving forces already present to have more effect. Better still is the effect of moving a hindering force so effectively that it becomes a driving force (i.e., it moves from lack of corporate support to total corporate support).

■ ## ISSUE 2 ■

Impact of Participative Management on Organizational Structure and Hierarchy

The potential success of participative management is affected by the nature of the organizational structure. Because *most* organizational structures are based on a value and belief system that differs from that of participative management, it is critical to examine that influence on a changed set of operational principles. Figure 3.2 compares the traditional structure to the assumptions underlying participative management.

Figure 3.2 does *not* assume that a hierarchy must be missing in order for participative management to be successful. There have been many successful applications of participative management by introducing it as a parallel process to existing structures. For example, General Electric Canada's Lighting Division introduced a concept of parallel "product teams." A team formed of representatives from each existing organizational unit decides on product strategy and implementation. A typical team might comprise:

- A product manager (e.g., from commercial fluorescent bulbs)

TRADITIONAL ORGANIZATION STRUCTURE	PARTICIPATIVE MANAGEMENT
• Top–down direction is required for control	• Top of organization provides leadership (i.e., vision, goals, support) • Control is shared with those who influence results
• Clear signing authorities and decision-making levels	• Shared decision making on some issues • Signing authorities meet legal requirements, not operating requirements
• Information is restricted to key people	• Information is necessary for operating people to do job and make decisions
• Specialization is key for job/work design	• Generalization (i.e., having multiple skills) is useful as well as specialization; the norm is "do what we need to do"
• Relationships between units need to be managed by appropriate levels	• Relationships between units need to be managed by those who need to interact
• Bottom of the organization exists to support the top	• Top of the organization exists to support the bottom (product/service/ producers)

FIGURE 3.2   BELIEFS/VALUES ABOUT STRUCTURE/HIERARCHY

- A production supervisor
- A maintenance supervisor
- A materials manager (production planning and purchasing)
- A marketing manager

- An account representative
- A distribution supervisor.

The organizational chart has not changed, but decisions are made in a more participative and effective manner by all involved in the product's sales, production, and distribution.

Some Thoughts on Approaching this Issue

Having worked with many organizations in Canada, the United States, and Europe, we have observed, worked with, and heard about hundreds of approaches to structure and hierarchy. What is fascinating is that they all may be appropriate. A key message is that there is *no* one best way to structure for participative management. Complications can result if consultants and gurus tell organizations how they must be structured to be successful.

Many readers have heard the statement, "Every journey must begin from where you are." The same point can be made for introducing participative management. Each road map will be different because each organization is starting from a different point and is making the trip for its own reasons. If participative management is introduced as a survival strategy, radical change to structure and short time frames are appropriate. If participative management is introduced as an enhancement strategy for a successful organization, less structural reform is needed and the pace can be less demanding. Beware of the sociotechnical consultants who tell clients the time frame must be long and slow. They frequently are extending the number of billable days.

In all cases, we assume that existing organizations are seeking a change. The key first step before attempting to making changes to the structure is to consider three sets of questions:

1. *Where are we now?*

   - What is our culture?
   - What was the basis for our current structure?
   - What is our driving force for change?
   - How supportive of change are our people?
   - What are our strengths?
   - What are our weaknesses?
   - What problems currently exist?

2. *Where do we want to be?*

   - What is the vision?
   - How complete is the vision?
   - Do people want to go there?
   - What happens if we don't go?
   - What is significantly different from current practices?

3. *What is the best way to get there?*

   - How much change is needed?
   - Can practices be changed without structure?
   - What priority exists on the change issue?
   - How much of the organization is affected?
   - Who should decide on changes?
   - How should they be approached?

- Is there a sequence of changes that makes sense?
- Can we check progress?

Summary

A wide range of approaches can be taken by organizations. These range from *total* structural reorganization to *parallel* processes occurring gradually beside the nonchanged organizational structure. In Chapter 4, we provide examples of some approaches taken by different organizations. Again, there is not one right way to organize for participative management. The nature of the business, the nature of the culture, and the rigidity of the opposition all determine how far to go in changing the organization.

Even without structural change, employees' empowerment and involvement can be increased. However, the size of the expected increase is influenced by the degree of change introduced. The inability to change the entire organization is not sufficient reason to refrain from empowering people.

■   **ISSUE 3**   ■

Resourcing a Participative Management Process

Chapter 2 addressed the issue of "free" participative management. Participative management needs to be resourced like any other business strategy, and this creates some problems for the organization. In a period when dollars are tight and budgets are scrutinized as never before, participative management is perceived as an added cost to an existing overstretched budget.

Clearly participative management must be treated as an operating expense of business, not as an additional expense. The
cost of participative management affects four cost areas (discussed more fully in the following section):

1. The cost of training employees, supervisors, and managers
   to act effectively within a participative management mode

2. The cost of providing the time for building and sharpening
   these skills (i.e., overtime)

3. The cost of time involved in holding team meetings and
   addressing issues that would have required less time if handled by an individual with designated authority or a policy
   manual

4. The cost of providing support services in the organization
   development or human resource functions to provide coaching and facilitation to increase the effectiveness of the participative management process.

The costs of the first three items revolve around the issue of
time. Consensus as a tool is used more frequently in the participative management process than in traditional organizations,
and team meetings to discuss issues and reach consensus are
time-consuming. Japanese management philosophy states, "We
in Japan take much longer than Americans to make decisions.
However, because of the nature of our process of involvement, we
make that decision only once." This is where the payoff and pay-
back result from participative management. Consensus should
be used only in those instances where consensus is required.
Even in Japan, an individual is given the power to shut down an
assembly line if he or she discovers a problem.

Some Approaches toward Resourcing Participative Management

If it is a valid process for increasing effectiveness in the organization, participative management must be strong enough to provide positive numbers on a cost–benefit analysis, just like any other management project or activity. We have mentioned repeatedly that participative management is a business decision. It is not an act of faith by managers on the basis that payoff comes from happy, involved people. Rather, it is a process that increases the effectiveness of the organization in terms of improved flexibility, quality, commitment, and utilization of resources. Before beginning a process of participative management, the organization must be willing to assess whether the problems to be overcome and the issues to be addressed warrant the cost of implementing such a process.

We previously indicated that it is possible to estimate the cost of participative management by categorizing the following three cost items:

1. *Training and skill building.* A budget is needed for the purchase of training, facilitation, and consultation to initiate participative management and to provide the base-level skills to begin the process. We are not saying that practicing consultants and trainers are a necessary component of participative management. However, our experience indicates that in the early stages of participative management, an outsider can be an effective lightning rod and motivate, encourage, and provide skills. The outsider also contributes objectivity and neutrality at the beginning of a change in attitudes and beliefs.

This cost should also include a travel budget to ensure that key people in the organization have a chance to visit other organizations currently using participative management processes. In some of the most successful applications of participative management, notably the Esso Chemical Canada plant in Sarnia, a significant budget was made available to ensure that operators, maintenance people, and process people were given the opportunity to visit organizations. Teams flew to Portland to visit Techtronics, or to Louisville to visit Bausch and Lomb. These visits included the opportunity for a maintenance person to talk to a maintenance person, and an operator to talk to an operator. Thus, staff get a clear, unbiased impression of the impact of participative management on the day-to-day life of workers. From an operator's point of view, external consultants are only one influence on their decision about whether participative management is the right way to go.

2. *Training administration cost.* Funds also should be allotted for training. The organization might choose to budget for conference rooms, hotel rooms, and meals for the initial training activities. These training costs can frequently amount to a significant sum of money. We have run sessions on team skills at some of the finest resorts in the world, as well as in local hotel rooms a few miles from a plant and in plant conference rooms on site. Management should consider whether choice of location is intended to represent a perceived reward. By no means, however, is it necessary that this budget figure get out of hand. Our experience indicates that in certain instances an off-site location can be an effective tool for team building because of the evening activities and opportunities for people to get to know each other in nonstructured situations. This can have a significant payoff.

We have also seen misused and abused training facility budgets, particularly when an organization decides to buy its way into participative management. One client consciously chose the best hotels within the area and arranged for hospitality suites for use by participants. The client also included extracurricular activities, such as bowling, golf, or some other team-based activity, to be charged back to the rooms. We believe it is not necessary to go to that extreme to introduce participative management. However, the feeling of total conspicuous consumption achieved significant benefit for that particular organization.

3. *Overtime.* The cost of overtime and coverage time for people involved in team activities also enters into the cost–benefit equation. Participative management is designed to enhance both the productivity and the quality of an organization. However, organizations cannot shut down to create this new way of working. When the necessary training and team meetings are occurring, production and services must continue. Consequently, the removal of key people for the development of the new process is a necessary added cost factor.

Organizations with shift-team operations have a range of responses. One client's belief in participative management is so strong that it is calculated into the cost of business, and overtime is provided for team meetings and training. As a result, it is much easier to get people involved in the initial stages of team development, particularly when they are receiving $45 per hour to sit in meetings and participate in training programs. However, this has increased the salary budget significantly during the first year of participative management introduction.

The Benefit Side of the Equation

In his book called *Quality is Free,* Phillip Crosby makes the point that, despite the time and costs involved in training people in statistical process, control, and other quality approaches, the payoff in terms of reduced rework, fewer rejects, and improved operating procedures far outweighs the costs. There is absolutely no question of the strong relationship between participative management and quality, and Crosby's arguments are relevant to participative management. One client in the petrochemical industry recently paid a $165,000 fine because of an environmental spill. Add the cost of spill cleanup and public relations in the community, and the cost becomes very significant. Investigations clearly identified that the spill was preventable and could have been avoided had any one of four individuals on the unit assumed responsibility. Each individual assumed that it was not his or her job and that someone higher up in the organization would recognize the danger and issue the appropriate orders to avoid the incident. Although this example was chosen at random to make a point, hundreds of these events occur weekly. Organizations now budget for spills, cleanups, product recalls, and customer complaints and build enough dollars into their budgets to handle acceptable failure rates.

A second benefit that should be considered is the ultimate reduction in overtime. Over the long term, participative management leads to a reduction to overtime hours in plants. This statement seems to conflict with an earlier statement that you must expect overtime during the introduction of the process. However, as participative management develops, the cross-training involved in people learning other people's jobs reduces the need for people to be called in for minor problems. In the petrochemical industry, for example, someone frequently is called in to do a half-hour setup at a minimum of six hours of double time. An on-site team member with the skills to do the half-hour job can save the company from the costly six hours at $50 per hour.

As we have emphasized, the goal of participative management is not to eliminate overtime. It is to reduce *unnecessary* overtime. Because of production requirements, pressures, and normal problems of running a business, overtime will always be a component of any manufacturing operation. However, a treasure trove exists in the reduction of unnecessary overtime caused by the failure of people to plan ahead or accept responsibility, and the failure of teams to accept responsibility for getting the product out.

Some Solutions for Reducing Cost Elements

The following are offered as solutions for reducing costs:

1. *Use of facilitators.* After 10 years of experience with participative management, we believe that the most effective means of introducing and maintaining a program is a blended approach of external and internal facilitators. In the early stages, external facilitators can be helpful in bringing about the fundamental skill-level base required for participative management. As mentioned earlier, outside facilitators draw on the experiences of other organizations and frequently bring a neutrality that allows discussion of issues that might not be dealt with by an internal facilitator. Let us be quite clear on this issue: The skill level difference between an internal and an external facilitator is not necessarily as great as many people think. Internal facilitators often can present the same programs as conducted by external facilitators. The issue is often the acceptability of an internal facilitator to the operating personnel because of his or her prior history in the organization.

Once a program has been launched and has provided base-level skills, internal facilitators can be used to provide the ongoing coaching and support when teams and groups face issues that training may not have prepared them for. At Esso Chemical Canada, we trained a core group of twelve internal facilitators.

Their jobs at the organization are irrelevant. What is important is that internal facilitators bring a skill they have developed in understanding group processes, providing neutral leadership, and giving a process to groups that may need assistance from someone external to that group. These people operate as facilitators as an add-on function to their job. Their facilitator duties range from 10 to 30 percent of their job activities. These employees are gaining a tremendous understanding of the problems and issues across the plant. From a career development standpoint, these people are being trained to lead groups effectively, understand processes, solve problems, and resolve conflict. They are being prepared to be future leaders of the organization. We very strongly recommend that, in resourcing participative management, a clear consideration be made about the choosing, using, and supporting of an internal base. This reduces the cost of and schedule dependency on external consultants.

2. *Emphasize work issues, not training.* Myth 2 dealt with the issue that participative management is not new. Therefore, it might be helpful in the consideration of resourcing participative management to not treat it as being new. There can easily be an inflated perception of the amount of training required before a team can begin to operate effectively as a team. We must assume that people have some skills to work together. One strategy we have used effectively in organizations is to focus on a few *key* team skills and minimize the amount of time we spend on classroom discussions, simulations, and other educational techniques. It is our intention that after one day of simulations, training, and discussions, people are able and willing to begin to work on some of the actual issues facing a team. Consequently, when we take a team away for three days of team building, it is our belief that at least two of those days should be used to work

actual issues rather than spending all three days in training exercises that build skills toward resolving real issues.

Training sessions should not be seen as exercises that replace doing *real* work. Actual work and real issues must be built into the training programs so that some progress toward a solution is made and not left to a team in a nontraining situation. In other words, to reduce the costs invested in training, you should focus on the key critical skills, get people working on real issues, and implant the additional skills as and when required. We frequently fail to give credit to teams with the ability to get on with the job, and we make assumptions about what we need to teach them before they are willing to work. This is a costly assumption in terms of resourcing participative management.

3. *Targeting as a resourcing strategy.* Another consideration is to use selective target development rather than blanketing the entire organization with equal training at the same time. Some organizations have approached participative management by mandating an introduction in which every person in the organization participated and learned the components, rationale, and techniques of participative management. Although we can understand this strategy in a small organization where there is constant integration among unit members, we question its validity, from a resourcing point of view, in a large organization.

Some organizations use a readiness factor to target parts of the organization that are ready and willing to move forward on participative management. These parts of the organization are then chosen to be the pilot or the lead in the participative management training focus. These people receive awareness skills as well as detailed team and team-effectiveness skills and begin to implement the process immediately. The rest of the organization can then observe and evaluate the effectiveness of the pilot organization. As success occurs, there is an increased readiness in the rest of the organization. When money is spent on developing skills, time between the cost of training and the application toward real work issues is shortened. Training is a very expensive proposition for organizations and should not be proposed as a total solution without having a specific strategy underlying it.

4. *Tracking and controlling.* Participative management should not be treated any differently from other management activities. You must monitor progress, track results, and keep control of costs. Freedom to participate and be involved in organizational decisions does not mean freedom from accountability in terms of the cost of that participation and involvement. We are shocked when we ask people how much they have spent on the participative management process and they throw up their hands and say, "Who knows?" Because of the element of trust built into the participative model, there is the possibility of abuse (conscious or unconscious) by some individuals in the organization. Abuse must be handled like any management issue in terms of confrontation, discussion, and negotiation. It must not be ignored, or it increases the perception that participative management is anarchy and is not being managed.

Summary

Participative management is not free. It *costs* and it *pays off.* It must be budgeted for, tracked, and managed. If, as a management team, you cannot justify the payoffs, then participative management should not be part of the strategy for your organization.

■ ISSUE 4 ■

Impact of Participative Management on Decision Making

Of the issues that participative management confronts, how decisions have been made in the organization is probably the most threatening. Fundamentally, participative management is about people who are involved in issues and have a role in resolving these issues. Executives and managers, who have traditionally made decisions without consultation or input, regard participative management as an unnatural process. Many executives have been taught, based on the quote from John G. Pollard, that executive ability is "deciding quickly and getting someone else to do the work."

Organizations have developed with a firm belief that stability is essential to good management. Being in control is valued as evidence of competent managerial behavior. Specifically, control over the decision-making process is the most fundamental prerogative of management, as represented by a rigid set of signing authorities and a clear separation of doing and thinking. Participative management attacks some of these basic beliefs and values. It assumes that everyone in the organization has the capacity to contribute to those issues that affect their responsibility. It assumes that people who do the job, know the job.

The issue facing organizations moving toward participative management is how to deal with "spectrum thinking," the thought process characterized by extreme pendulum swings. Managers may have made all the decisions before, but employees/teams make all the decisions in participative management. As in all examples of spectrum thinking, the truth usually lies somewhere in the middle. Participative management creates expectations for involvement and participation, and these expectations that need to be managed. Participative management assumes a clear definition of decision-making responsibility. As mentioned in Myth 5, participative management is about defining:

- Which decisions should be made by a team or empowered individuals.
- Which decisions should be made by a specific team/individual, but *must* involve collaboration prior to finalization.
- Which decisions should be made independent of input/involvement.

There is no easy involvement formula for participative management. Each situation requires consideration regarding the proper way for that decision to be made.

Reasons to Address the Decision-Making Process

People make up organizations. They make decisions and are affected by changes in the decision-making process. Decision making is the basis of participative management. If everything else in participative management is put in place, but no alterations are made in the decision-making process, you do not have participative management.

Additionally, changes in the decision-making process create a variety of reactions from the people in the system. Many top managers feel challenged and unsure of how to be effective leaders when decisions are shared. Middle managers are confused because of the change in their role and concerned by the incessant pronouncements of writers who forecast the end of the middle manager. Supervisors are threatened because of the need to ask rather than tell. Employees are skeptical about what they are supposed to do and unsure of how to go about doing it. External suppliers, customers, and others who relate to the organization, are confused about who has authority to do what. For these reasons, the introduction of participative management requires a conscious and diligent assessment and plan to modify the decision-making process.

Some Approaches to the Decision-Making Process

As practicing participative management consultants, we have neither developed our skills and knowledge through abstract conceptualization, nor developed original theories that are breakthroughs in participative management. Rather, we are "learning sponges." We are the product of what we read, experience, and learn from talking to others. The result is a stew, not a smorgasbord of individual ideas. It is often difficult to identify the exact source of an inspiration that helps a group out of an impasse or directs them to a successful resolution. However, several sources dominate our approach, and credit must be given to them, even if they no longer recognize what we have done to their ideas.

First, in the field of decision involvement, responsibility, and styles, we have learned from Robert Tannenbaum and Warren Schmidt (*Harvard Business Review,* 1954) and a later variation on their work by Victor Vroom and Philip Yetton (*Leadership and Decision Making,* University of Pittsburgh Press, 1971). These authors clearly identified the situational approach to decision making, which we regard as the cornerstone of participative management.

Second, Edward Lawler (*High Involvement Management,* Josey-Bass, 1986) extended our thinking to include a mode of effectiveness for participation in organizational decision making. Lawler wrote that participation (decision making) is a function of four key elements, of which must exist:

1. Information base and flow to ensure that proper information is available to make decisions

2. Knowledge and skills in how to make decisions

3. Power and authority to make decisions (i.e., empowerment)

4. Rewards to encourage accepting responsibility to make decisions.

In pursuing Lawler's logic, organizations must address whether they are willing to ensure that all four elements are given to individuals/teams in the organization.

Compensating Systems

If there is not a total commitment to self-directed teams, provided with all four of Lawler's elements, then there is a need to establish compensating systems in the organization to allow for a more limited form of participative management. These compensating systems are discussed in the following sections. To be absolutely clear—we do not believe that self-directed teams are the only form of participative management.

Information Flow/Data Base

This element cannot be avoided. Just as managers cannot make effective decisions with poor or no data, groups cannot either.

Without a willingness to provide data or access to data, there should be no further discussion of participative management.

Most people in organizations do not have adequate information to contribute as effectively as they, and the organization's management, would like them to. Well-documented reasons range from managers who hoard information so they can maintain power and control to managers who don't know and never think to ask what information employees need that would help them participate more effectively in carrying out the work of the organization.

Sharing information with employees is a key factor in participative management. It builds trust between managers and employees, reduces the time people waste trying to get information necessary to their work, and results in higher quality decisions by the total organization. One interesting side-effect we have seen is that the sharing of information with employees results in managers getting higher quality information from within the organization, thus increasing their own effectiveness.

Find out what employees need and want to know about the organization's business, and give the information to them. If you have doubts, we suggest giving them more than you think they need; they will tell you what they don't want or need. Many managers worry that sharing some information with employees will result in leaks to their competitors. Our experience leads us to believe that nothing is further from the truth. The real truth is that industry competitors already know a lot about your business through other means, and more importantly, your employees have a vested interest in the organization's well-being in the marketplace. At Esso Chemical Canada's Sarnia plant, there is a stated value regarding this subject: "Open, honest, two-way communications between all levels on all topics." With the single exception of personal data, this openness is practiced actively throughout the site and has paid off handsomely in many ways. We suggest information sharing as a great place to start the participative management process because it opens the organization's collective mind to innovations in the workplace, and can very quickly help the organization to gain focus for the process.

The power and information grid presented in Figure 3.3 describes the relationship of empowerment and information. A requirement for good decision making is that authority/power is tempered by quality information. In traditional organizations, the largest boxes are boxes 2 and 3, as represented in Figure 3.4. Workers have the most current and in-depth information, but authority and power remain with managers. One goal of participative management is to enlarge the size of box 4. Assuming that the skill and willingness exist, *all* decisions should be made in box 4. The nature of the decision determines who makes the decision; however, information is the dominant factor, not

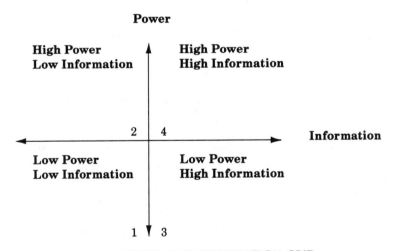

FIGURE 3.3   POWER AND INFORMATION GRID

Power

High Power
Low Information

- *These people typically are managers in a traditional organization*

- *These people can be dangerous since power without information leads to "bad" decisions.*

High Power
High Information

- *The goal of participative management is to ensure that all decisions are based on full data basis.*
- *The persons with the data should be empowered.*
- *This is where decisions should be made.*

2   4   Information

Low Power
Low Information

- *These employees should be informed about decisions.*
- *Unless information/power increases, they will simply be followers.*

Low Power
High Information

- *The unempowered employee in a traditional organization.*
- *These people have high frustration because of absence of power, high degree of questioning decisions, and low commitment to decisions.*

1   3

FIGURE 3.4   SAMPLE ANALYSIS OF TRADITIONAL ORGANIZATION

the person's level in the organization. A further example of the grid applied to a hospital organization is present in Figure 3.5.

Knowledge and Skills

In the short term, it is likely that a team will need to learn decision-making processes. This cannot be delegated; it must

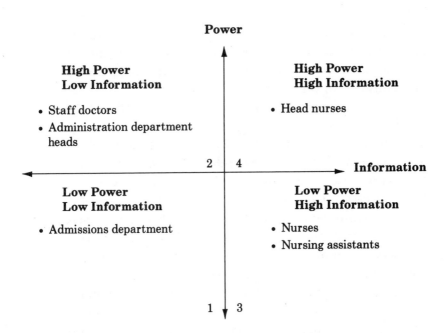

Power

High Power
Low Information

- Staff doctors
- Administration department
  heads

High Power
High Information

- Head nurses

2 | 4   **Information**

Low Power
Low Information

- Admissions department

Low Power
High Information

- Nurses
- Nursing assistants

1 | 3

FIGURE 3.5   SAMPLE ANALYSIS WITHIN A HOSPITAL ENVIRONMENT

be learned. To compensate for a group's lack of knowledge or skills, some organizations provide several compensating tools.

1. *Decision-making formats.*   Structured discussion sequences lead a team through the necessary steps of a decision-making process. They could be based on a Kepner-Tregoe approach, an Alamo Learning Systems approach, or any of several approaches to systematic decision making.

2. *Trained facilitators.*   These facilitators have a responsibility for guiding teams through the steps of a decision-making process. These are usually internal employees who have been specially trained to guide teams through different group processes without assuming control.

Many of our clients have chosen to use facilitators to increase the effectiveness of team problem-solving and decision-making skills. Not surprisingly, organizations approach the use of facilitators in very dissimilar ways.

Esso Chemical Canada's Sarnia plant introduced the use of facilitators as a means of helping teams with the group process. The facilitators focus on the clear understanding of the team effectiveness model (see Appendix III). The facilitator's job is to observe, listen, provide feedback, and guide the process. Some of Esso's most successful facilitators are operators, pipe fitters, maintenance specialists, and other hourly personnel. This role consumes 5 to 20 percent of the employees' time. Rick Chappel, coordinator of these facilitators, has the critical role of ensuring the successful use of resources.

A key principle that seems to work for Esso is that facilitators do not assume the role of facilitator for their own teams. Familiarity not only breeds contempt, but it also interferes with the objectivity required to be successful.

Nova Petrochemicals has developed a slightly different approach to the use of facilitators. They have linked facilitators to the organizational thrust of quality management with a workshop curriculum that includes the following stages:

1. Developing interactive skills—A four-day workshop focusing on specific interpersonal behaviors.

2. Quality management—A one-day introduction to the key elements of Nova's total quality approach.

3. Managing participation—A two-day workshop focusing on the essential skills of teams and group behaviors.

4. Managing situation improvement—A five-day workshop focusing on the specific skills of situational assessment,

problem solving, decision making, and creative problem solving.

5. Facilitating situation improvement—A four-day workshop aimed at providing skills in guiding and directing teams in the core processes of the previous stage.

Parallel programs are available on the topics of effective meeting skills (two days) and total quality awareness (four days). Nova uses facilitators more on an issues basis than on the team development process.

Martin Marietta, in Denver, has evolved a variation on the use of facilitators. The thrust at Martin Marietta is threefold:

1. Total quality is of paramount importance.

2. Teams are a critical parallel organizational component.

3. Empowerment goes along with innovation.

Martin Marietta launched an intensive quality program that ensured that attitude and skills were developed to the highest possible level. This was followed by an organization-wide team development program that increased the awareness of the power of teams. A steering committee established clear guidelines that empowered improvement teams to implement actions without a formal review process.

This training was supplemented by an organization-wide innovation skills program that provided teams with specific tools to generate innovative solutions. At this stage, facilitators were developed and used. The improvement teams were self-established and were aware of the limits to their mandate. Because these teams had yet to be trained in team skills, there was a need for a facilitator to assist them in addressing issues.

Martin Marietta has recognized a critical "truth" of participation. It is a "two-wave" phenomenon. The first wave is unleashing the enthusiasm and power of individuals/teams who are given freedom to improve situations that have been around for years. This first wave of activity was the basis for quality-circle success in many organizations (see Figure 3.6). The first wave recognizes that "enthusiasm and freedom when aimed at the obvious" pay dividends. However, when the easily identified issues are resolved, there is a decline in payoff and success.

The second wave (Figure 3.7) must be consciously introduced based on something stronger than enthusiasm. Martin Marietta identified the need to provide their teams with an in-depth approach to the more difficult situations. The needed skill was creative problem solving and was introduced with facilitators as a means of ongoing support.

Facilitators exist to guide teams, not to become team leaders. To be effective, facilitators bring the following skills to a team:

- An ability to understand group/team dynamics
- An ability to accept individual and team differences

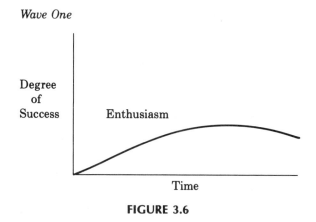

FIGURE 3.6

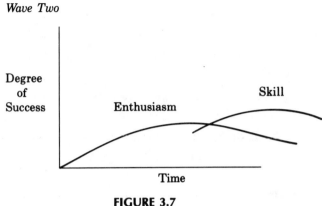

FIGURE 3.7

- An ability to suggest various processes that will help teams achieve their goal
- An ability to direct those processes
- An ability to help teams confront situations and accept responsibility for individual and team behavior.

Facilitators are an effective compensating tool for organizations that are transferring self-managing skills and abilities to teams. However, they are transitional and should not be institutionalized. One chemical plant became so dependent on facilitators that meetings were postponed until facilitators could be available.

Compensating Systems for Empowerment

Instant empowerment is impossible for most teams and individuals. The "flush of freedom" can create some very unexpected results, including the following:

- Refusals to accept empowerment
- Abuses of freedom (e.g., taking advantage of the system)
- Acceptance of empowerment followed by abandonment of responsibility
- Myopic focus on the empowered issues to the detriment of maintaining the ongoing system
- Systematic destruction of manager/employee relationships by using empowerment as a weapon against managers.

All these results were caused by a too hasty and ill-planned change from an autocratic system to participative management. Many successful examples of implementing empowerment have included a planned progression and the development of specific compensating systems to manage the transition to empowerment. Some of the compensating systems include the following:

1. *Top–down empowerment.* An unempowered manager cannot empower his or her employees/teams. It is difficult to give away what you do not have. For this reason, many organizations begin a systematic "cascade" of empowerment from the top down. The plant manager empowers department heads, the department heads empower section heads, and finally teams/individuals are empowered. This process helps protect both teams and managers from overreactions. The down side to this strategy is the extended time frame perceived by people at the bottom. The slowness creates a perception of lack of trust. For this reason, the cascading strategy can be combined with a selective empowerment approach.

2. *Empowerment from simplicity to complexity.* This strategy is based on the principle of growth fostered by success. With some clients, we have consciously identified and

selected extremely low-risk, fairly simple decisions as the initial team/individual tasks. Teams are empowered to make decisions within their skill and readiness limits. As the team becomes more skillful, confident, and willing to enlarge its scope for authority, the team is given new and more complex decisions for resolution. In one instance at a Shell refinery, the newly formed teams were vested with the power to devise team names. Although this task sounds trivial, it represented the decision level with which the teams were able to cope. Some teams had difficulty with this task. Today, after five years, the same teams are empowered to call out contractors, authorize overtime, select their own team coordinator, and make many other difficult, high-impact decisions.

3. *Use of steering committees.* In Chapter 4, we describe the role of steering committees, but a few words here describe their role as a compensating system for empowerment. Steering committees frequently operate as a "safety valve" for the degree of empowerment vested in teams. Rather than fully vesting power in a team, the steering committee retains a review role for critical decisions. If the steering committee carries out its role properly, it also ensures that the limitations of empowerment are clearly understood by the team. Empowerment is not an all-or-nothing issue. It almost always has boundaries that limit the degree of freedom. This creation and communication of boundaries represent a critical compensating system for empowerment.

Compensating Systems for Rewards

Ed Lawler's thesis that empowerment requires recognition of a need to reward people for accepting increased responsibility is beyond challenge. There is a naive, incorrect belief by some managers that empowerment is its own reward. As with our statement that there is no compensating system for information, we believe the same is true for the rewards issue. If an organization is not willing to openly and fundamentally change its basis for rewarding people, it should forget about empowerment. There is no compensating system.

■   **ISSUE 5**   ■

Impact of Participative Management Process on Roles

We have found that in the participative management process, key roles often are left unclear, undefined, or even unknown. Although roles change and evolve over the course of the change process, the evolution, like the change process itself, can and should be executed in a planned way. This issue is critical because changing roles are central to the introduction and implementation of participative management in any organization. Many problems we see in participative management implementation stem from this issue. We see the following problems on a recurring basis, but there are many others not mentioned here.

The Impact of Disempowered People

The most common problem we see is that key players at the first-line supervisory level are disempowered and seemingly devalued by managers who are eager to have participative management in place quickly. We call this the "Action Now! Syndrome." Managers unconsciously bypass supervisors, and in some cases simply take over the supervisor's role in working with employees. Although they have good intentions, they use bad tactics. (See

Chapter 6 for a more in-depth discussion of issues for the supervisor.) The results of these actions are well known:

- Employees begin to bypass supervisors.
- Supervisors lose self-esteem.
- Supervisors begin to resist participative management and suffer dire consequences for their resistance.
- Employees and managers begin to wonder whether supervisors are the major impediment to participative management.
- Some supervisors may even be removed from their positions and replaced.
- Good employees refuse promotions to supervision.
- Managers begin to wonder if supervisors are necessary at all.

This last point often leads to the self-fulfilling prophecy about leaderless teams. In the more severe cases, we have seen a total failure of the participative management process and a return to the control mode of management.

Abdication of Authority

The second major problem caused by this issue (with some other contributing factors) is the abdication of authority by managers. The cause is almost universal: Managers fear they might alienate employees and lose their support for participative management, so they back away from their role in the decision-making process at critical points in the process. As a result of this abdication, some necessary structures and systems may be removed or replaced too early—or worse, they may be removed and not replaced at all—leaving employees at all levels wondering about the logic and viability of participative management.

Too often, participative management is misinterpreted as permissive management, which leads to confusion, frustration, and even chaos. In every organization, there are a few "me first" people who abuse the system. When abdication occurs, the message may be sent that it is okay to get what you can for yourself because managers don't care. "Me first" people will flourish under these conditions.

Why It Is Important to Deal with the Issue

Defining roles in the participative management process, in clear terms, facilitates the successful implementation of participative management. It is not restrictive or hindering as some people believe. In an organization with a history of control management that is setting out on the road to participative management, it is important for people to understand that it will not be an overnight success. Roles evolve as the organization gains in experience and skill maturity. If people are accustomed to working under a control style of management, they probably do not have the skills to take on many of the responsibilities participative management will require of them. They also have a certain level of comfort in knowing that someone will tell them what to do, as well as how and when to do it. In most cases, paternalistic or maternalistic organizations take good care of employees, and giving this up can create resistance.

Managers can help the organization avoid some of the confusion, frustration, and uncertainty mentioned earlier, and should even explain how roles are intended to change over time, as clearly as possible. There is enough confusion, frustration, and uncertainty in the transition to participative management without adding to them by ignoring the issue of roles. There are some excellent models and techniques available for defining changing roles in the participative management process, and a number of excellent consultants are happy to extend their services in this area. A model we have used for years, and which seems to fit for role definition, is a decision-making model developed by Victor Vroom and Phillip Yetton (University of Pittsburgh Press, 1971). We have modified the model for use with our clients, and it has worked well in clarifying planning and implementation processes. It also has brought sighs of relief in some organizations, and increased the comfort level of many managers when they learn they will always have responsibility for some organizational decisions. (See Appendix II for a more detailed definition of the managing participation model.)

How to Deal with this Issue

It is tempting to be prescriptive, given our combined experience, but every organization is unique and starts its journey to participative management from a different place in terms of existing roles. Instead, we share a technique developed by Dick Beckard and Reuban Harris that has been invaluable to us in helping organizations work through this issue in a way that makes sense to everyone. We also provide a list of role descriptions that appear to be most common in organizations with participative management systems.

Richard Beckard and Reuban Harris, in a book entitled *Organization Transitions* (Addison-Wesley, Reading, Mass, 1977), describe a technique they appropriately call "responsibility charting." The technique helps define the roles of key players in the decision-making process. We recommend its use following these steps:

1. Using the statement of vision we mentioned earlier in this chapter, determine the anticipated role of each key player in the decision-making process. Because there are literally thousands of decisions made in any organization, we suggest the use of categories (e.g., hiring new employees, promoting employees, setting operating goals, developing budgets). This keeps the number of roles to a manageable size yet gives a broad picture. Apply a liberal dose of logic. For example, it is unlikely that many organizations will involve operating employees in the selection of product range or market niche decisions. These decisions are, and likely will continue to be, the domain of senior managers.

2. Define the roles of the same key players in today's organizational context. This gives a good sense of how far the organization has to move before participative management is truly implemented.

3. After gaining a clear picture of your present and end state roles, identify the skills, knowledge, information, and authority levels required for today's key players to take on the responsibilities that will be theirs in the future. You can set short-term goals for people in the organization to begin to take on these new responsibilities. The plan needs to be sequential in nature and evolutionary. Too much too soon will put too much stress on employees; too little, and they may regard their work as mundane and unimportant to the organization. One way to counteract this perception is to ensure that employees, or their representatives, are involved in this exercise. They have a good sense of how much expansion they can handle, and they probably will surprise most managers by asking for more responsibility sooner. One employee goal in participative management is more freedom from managerial control. Therefore, we believe that managers and employees must agree on how to move responsibility from managers to employees in an acceptable way.

Roles in Participative Management

We have seen a variety of roles emerge as organizations move to participative management. However, there appears to be a standard set of roles common to all organizations. The following sections briefly describe the common roles that support the participative management process.

The Senior Manager

The senior manager has the central role in the participative management process, which must have committed leadership from the top. The multiple roles played by this individual are indispensable, and without this person's involvement, most participative management efforts are a waste of time and resources. This manager's primary role is that of *visionary leader:* The vision belongs to, and is created by, this individual. He or she, more than anyone else in the organization, must behave according to the values and beliefs contained in the vision.

The *champion* is the true change agent in the organization. He or she *sponsors* major activities aimed at achieving participative management through the collective efforts of employees. In some instances, the roles of sponsor and champion reside in two different positions, which is worth addressing here. The champion requires strong political skills needed for selling participative management as a sound business strategy, both within and outside the organization. He or she is also the keeper of the values associated with participative management and must personally practice those values while auditing the behaviors of others in the organization to ensure adherence to the values. The sponsor role, on the other hand, commits the organization's resources to the activities associated with participative management. In some cases, the champion does not have sufficient control or authority to obtain the necessary resources to carry out the plans for participative management and may have to go outside his or her immediate domain to obtain sponsorship from someone farther up in the organization.

The *boundary manager* is crucial to participative management. Many participative management efforts have been started in operating plants or departments of large organizations with little or no support from the central organization or head office. In some cases, the strongest resistance comes from the central organization, which may view the impact of participative management on its work as negative. If employees are going to be involved in the management of the business, then change is going to affect the way central functions interface with operations, perhaps creating more work for those in the central function roles. Boundary management means gaining acceptance for participative management from key executives who manage the central functions, which requires increased communication and negotiation of new rules to resolve interface issues in the future. A skilled boundary manager tries to get active support from central functions that directly affect his or her operation (i.e., sales and marketing). Barring that, the boundary manager must take appropriate actions to create a neutral situation. This is the minimum requirement for the organization to proceed with participative management. Boundary management is a difficult and sometimes time-consuming role. We recommend that managers develop a strategy for playing this role, or be prepared for some unpleasant surprises in the future. We have seen situations where this role was not attended to early enough, and the resultant actions by powerful people in central functions literally brought participative management to a halt. In one extreme case, an operation was sold off because participative management could not be dismantled and people in powerful central positions felt the plant culture was in total conflict with the corporate culture. As we said, this was an extreme case, but it points out the importance of this role and the need for proactive thought and action.

The *decision maker and approver* is most important in the initial stages of participative management implementation. The senior manager, as custodian of participative management, must ensure that decisions, programs, and activities that are undertaken do not violate the values and principles associated with participative management and that all actions will move the organization closer to the vision. This should not be construed as meaning that decisions, programs, and activities must be exactly as the senior manager would design them (i.e., another form of control management which we call "read my mind"). This role's primary objective is to ensure that the change plan is proceeding along the agreed upon path to participative management.

Finally, the senior manager plays the role of participant in the participative management process because he or she is a stakeholder in the outcome, and the change will have a major impact on his or her work in the future. The senior manager has some vital input to the participative management process and to decisions that affect the total organization. Therefore, he or she should participate, not as the chairperson, but as a full member in those decisions, with equal rights and responsibilities for influencing the outcomes. Because subordinate managers are normally involved in organization-wide decisions (or they should be), the senior manager's involvement has the added feature of creating opportunities for modeling the kind of behavior participative management requires of managers. (In Chapter 6, we discuss the leadership issues.)

Steering Committee

We believe the role of the steering committee in participative management is so significant that it needs to be thought of as second only to the senior manager in the hierarchy of the organization. The committee's role should determine the membership, but in our experience, this committee works best when its membership includes the formal and informal leadership of the organization and its various employee groups.

The central role of the steering committee, as its name implies, is to *guide* the participative management process through implementation. This often means addressing issues that may hinder participative management; developing the roles and mandates for subcommittees; keeping abreast of developments and progress toward the vision; ensuring consistency of activities between departments where it makes sense to be consistent; and deciding on questions such as pace and timing of the different phases of implementation. A second role of the committee is that of *sponsor* for major activities that require the expenditure of internal resources over which the organization has total discretionary power. A third role is that of proposal *evaluator and approver.* In this role, the committee judges the appropriateness and applicability of various change proposals emanating from other bodies within the organization. The fourth role for the steering committee is that of *sensor* of the organization's well-being; that is, the steering committee regularly senses and evaluates, both formally and informally, how employees are responding to the changes that are occurring—sometimes many changes in parallel at a rapid pace—and judges whether to take corrective actions. It is easy, in the highly energetic process of moving forward, to overlook the demands on employees at all levels. It may be wise and necessary to "slow down to speed up."

Fewer activities with higher results are always better than many activities with spotty results.

Finally, the steering committee *integrates* the interests of many diverse groups and ensures that the process results in equity and balance. If participative management is perceived to be a "rob Peter to pay Paul" process, disgruntled groups will consciously or unconsciously block its implementation and cause rifts in the organization. For example, some organizations like to use the "pilot project" approach, which is to try it in a small unit or department and, if it works there, apply it in other units. We call this the toe-in-the-water approach. In cases we have seen, this approach has led to strong negative reactions from other units which felt the pilot group was trying to usurp power and authority. There is a case for pilot projects, but the steering committee needs to be very proactive in resolving potential interface problems before they arise. An effective steering committee will almost always predict accurately where and what problems will arise, and it can also determine effective plans for counteracting those problems.

Middle Managers

The role of middle managers in the participative management process is similar to that of the senior manager, but on a different scale. Within his or her own part of the organization, each middle manager must *lead champion,* and *sponsor* the implementation activities associated with participative management. He or she must be a *critical supporter* of the vision and the process, and must *translate* the vision into terms that the unit can understand and subscribe to in concrete ways. Finally, the middle manager must be a *coach and mentor* for first-line supervisors to ensure that they have the correct balance of attitudes, skill, and knowledge to carry out their changing role in the participative management process.

First-Line Supervisors

In our view, the first-line supervisor is as crucial as the senior manager to the success of the change process in participative management. This is the only individual in management who interfaces with employees on a regular basis. He or she probably understands employees' needs and wants better than any other level of management. Consequently, a critical role becomes that of *facilitator,* that is, identifying and solving issues with the work force as they implement participative management together. In addition, the first-line supervisor plays the role of *coach* and *mentor* to the employees, just as the middle manager does for him or her. Finally, we must remember that the first-line supervisor is a full member in the process, with equal rights and equally valuable opinions and ideas.

Employee Representatives

The major role of employee representatives is to *negotiate* changes on behalf of their constituents, that is to negotiate *how* to implement changes rather than *whether* changes are necessary. This is often a difficult role to play, as the majority of employees will agree with the concepts of participative management. However, some small but influential groups always feel threatened by the change, and these are the groups for which employee representatives will be asked to negotiate special consideration. In these cases, managers need to be especially sensitive to the issues and work with the employee representatives to find win–win solutions, while maintaining constancy and fairness in the process.

Another role of employee representatives is that of *process auditor* to ensure that managers and employees behave in accordance with the stated vision and values. In this role, they can be invaluable to the total organization, particularly early in the process, and bring hard-to-get data to the steering committee (i.e., data about what is really happening in the organization). Of course, all this assumes a healthy level of trust between the organization's management and the employee representatives. A third role for this group is to work with managers to *identify and resolve* organization-wide issues that affect the total work force, not only those employees they represent.

Participative management is for everyone, not only a select group, and employee representatives may have some very creative and innovative input on bringing unrepresented groups into the participative management process. Finally, employee representatives play the role of *partner* in the participative management process. In our experience, when participative management succeeds or fails, both managers and employee representatives reap the harvest equally. Both win or lose based on actions they take in partnership. It is understandable that some unions resist and often reject outright the notion of joining with management in the implementation of participative management. The stakes are high.

Employees

Last, but far from least, are the people who actually make participative management happen: the employees. Their major role is that of *contributor*. If participative management is effectively implemented, their contribution to the organization can be significantly enhanced. In return, their knowledge, skill, and degree of autonomy should also be enhanced. Many organizations are finding that participative management also leads naturally to work redesign, in which case employees play the role of *work designers*. This can effectively result in higher wages as they take on more managerial-type tasks; however, we caution against using this as a motivator. Unless you are moving directly to a form of gain or profit sharing, both of which use formulas to compute the employee's share of return for effort, then you can only guess, probably inaccurately, at what employees might gain monetarily from any work redesign activity. Don't promise anything you might not be able to deliver.

SUMMARY

We have described the roles in the participative management process as we have experienced them in our work. In our view, these roles need to be addressed early in the process to clarify what the roles are expected to be in the future and what they are today, and to begin planning an orderly transition from present to future roles. By doing so, we believe that many organizations can avoid a great deal of unnecessary frustration, conflict, and cost along the way to participative management.

4

ISSUES FOR
TEAMS/GROUPS

Participative management is normally implemented through teams, groups, task forces, and other conglomerations of people. To participate means to interact, share in, take part in. In organizations, participation can be with peers, suppliers, superiors, or subordinates. The interaction can be one-on-one or within a team/group structure. The ultimate effectiveness of participative management often is determined not by how well an organization addresses its issues, but by how well the operational work groups make operating decisions, and identify and resolve their issues. Participative management is not necessarily restricted to the use of teams; however, teams seem to be the dominant manifestation of participative management. This chapter explores some of the team issues we have encountered. Again, all issues can not be covered, because every team is unique and meets a unique set of issues. Thus, we have chosen to discuss the most common or most contentious issues.

As stated elsewhere in this book, teams are not new. The use of teams can be traced back to Moses organizing the Israelites for their flight from Egypt. Military structure is based on the breakdown of armies into discrete functional units. Many sports are played with teams. Even individual sports, such as golf, sometimes become team competitions.

Teams exist in all organizations, with or without participative management. Participative management challenges teams in the following ways:

- Structure
- Makeup
- Degree of empowerment (or freedom to act)

- Processes
- Goals
- Leadership and membership roles in existing teams.

The organization has to focus on two distinct issues in relation to the use of teams:

1. Reviewing and assessing existing teams to determine what, if anything, has to be done to integrate them into a participative management philosophy. These are usually functional teams.

2. Identifying new teams required to ensure that participative management is successful across the whole organization. These new teams are usually cross-functional or task forces created to manage overlaps and integration.

In this chapter, we attempt to identify the processes necessary to provide teams with the road map for success. Of equal importance is the issue of when to use teams and when to avoid the use of teams. Over the years, we have encountered managers who have tried to create teams that were doomed to failure because the use of teams was inappropriate for the task at hand.

IF TEAMS ARE THE ANSWER, WHAT WAS THE QUESTION?

Teams are or should be an organizational response to the need to achieve a specific set of objectives. They are not useful as ends in themselves. For teams to be the answer, the following criteria need to exist in an organization:

1. A specific activity needs attention and achievement.

2. The goal or objective requires the input of multiple resources.

3. The achievement of the goal requires commitment from the involved parties.

4. The achievement of the goal cannot be met without interdependency.

Interdependency

The basic difference between a work group and a work team is interdependency. Individual members working alone cannot achieve the agreed upon goal without the ongoing interaction with others who share the same goal. If one person can get the job done *without* another's efforts, the two can work together, but they are not a team.

A Customer Service Team

For example, a customer service repair specialist is a critical individual for a large appliance manufacturing organization. The regional offices comprise a customer service supervisor, an inventory supervisor, a dispatcher/scheduler, a number of warehouse personnel, and a larger number of customer service repair specialists. Although there are obvious dependency relationships among the inventory supervisor, the customer service supervisor, and the dispatcher, the repair specialists operate independently. Each day they receive their work orders, parts, and trucks and disappear into the residential neighborhoods for eight hours of uninterrupted individual relationships with customers and appliances. To force a team concept on the repair specialists would be futile and counterproductive.

This does not mean that participative management cannot be used. Morning meetings prior to work assignments can be used for information sharing, input on policies and practices, proposals about changes, and other important uses of the specialists' knowledge and skills.

However, no person is an island in any organization. The field repair specialist depends on accurate dispatch information, and proper inventory procedures to ensure that the right parts are available at the right time. Because customer service is the ultimate goal for this part of the organization, it is critical that the team concept *support* the repair specialist. This sounds contradictory, since we said earlier that teams were not appropriate. To be clear, we are stating that a team of *interdependent* repair specialists is inappropriate. However, the development of a *cohesive* team of three key players—dispatch, inventory, and repair specialists—is achievable. In this team, the "star" is the repair specialist. Everyone else *supports* the customer interface. As Ron Zemke states in *Service America,* (Warner Books, N. Y., 1985) "If you are not servicing the customer you should be servicing someone who is!"

The concept of a star creates a problem for some people. There is a myth of equality that exists around participative management. The reality is that stars do exist because a prime person is needed to influence the team's goal. The role should be functionally created, not ego created. In football, the quarterback handles the ball on every play. The execution of the offensive strategy is built entirely around the quarterback's ability to carry out his or her role. Because of the interdependence issue, the star must operate with the support of the teammates. A call for equality in football would mean that everyone would take turns handling the snap from center. It would make for interesting viewing of football, but we wouldn't bet on that team's ability to win.

How teams work is the focus of Chapter 5. Some of the above issues should become clearer as the process of team effectiveness is explored. Before looking at how teams work, however, we need to define what we mean by teams.

TEAMS, GROUPS, AND OTHER MOTLEY CREWS

Participative management is about focused behavior. It is about people working together to achieve commonly shared goals, and is not necessarily restricted to teams, because there are many other ways that people can work together. Effective organizations use a wide range of options in structuring the work–people relationship. The key is to understand the differences, however subtle, of the various forms of people participation alignment. With clarity comes realistic expectations and an ability to support and reward people who work together.

Some people will see this issue as an exercise in semantics. Perhaps they are right. Words play a critical part in our ability to understand and effectively manage issues. For example, a group that operates effectively yet gets measured by the standards of a team will ultimately lose its effectiveness since a group and a team are measured against quite different criteria and expectations.

Why Use Teams or Groups

The accepted belief, with some validation, is that a team of people can in fact produce a better result than can individual contributors. The principle of synergy assumes that a number of people meeting together and discussing a situation have a greater overall impact than a number of individuals who approach a situation independently. This belief is based on several key factors:

- Different people will bring different information or data bases, which will create a more complete picture or provide new and different insights to the problem.
- The interaction of these people will create a combined data base that exceeds each individual's input.
- In the complexities of most tasks, the ultimate implementation will be carried out by more than one person. The awareness of the total picture allows people to cooperatively plan independent behavior so that it leads toward the common good or the common goal.
- There is a greater cost-effectiveness to bringing a team of four people together and addressing an issue than there would be in independently gathering four individual inputs.

Types of Teams and Groups

People who work together are not necessarily teams. Organizations structure all sorts of groupings of people to achieve their objectives. To be successful in assigning groupings, it is critical to understand the nature of those groupings. Only by having a clear understanding of the type of group structure we create, can we set realistic expectations for that group of people.

There are five typical forms of organizational structures in most organizations:

1. Natural work groups

2. Natural work teams

3. Integrated work teams

4. Short-term task forces

5. Long-term committees

The first three are internal to the organizational chart; the last two are parallel to the organizational chart. All these forms have the potential for use in a participative management structure, but all are slightly different. In the following sections, we describe each and compare the similarities and differences. A summary chart is found in Appendix V.

NATURAL WORK GROUPS

Establishing natural work groups is the traditional approach to creating many organizational units within a typical organizational chart. It is the grouping of individuals and clusters into a structure that is convenient for managing. The individuals or clusters may or may not have an interdependency relationship. The organization has a great need to ensure that each activity fits under an umbrella. Thus, jobs and functions are combined and given a common title. For example, one organization may divide functions into the following departments: accounting, human resources, sales, and customer repair. Each department is conveniently managed by one person who tries to create a common goal and focus for independent subunits.

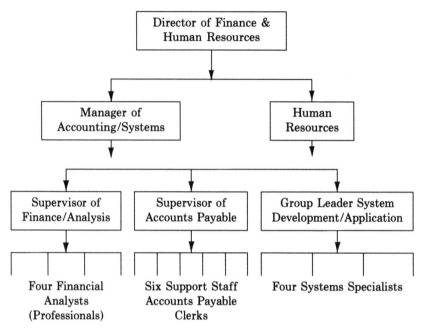

FIGURE 4.1   ACCOUNTING DEPARTMENT ORGANIZATION CHART

To elaborate, we examine the accounting department of a multinational chemical organization. This staff function supports the petrochemical site of 600 people. The company is organized on a business/product-line basis with three independent business managers, each running his or her own chemical business on a common site. Certain centralized service functions exist to support the separate produce lines. The current organizational chart of the department is shown in Figure 4.1.

Except for the system development/application group, this seems to be a logical organizational structure. Even the system group has a responsibility for developing and maintaining financial reporting and tracking systems. However, it doesn't take a rocket scientist to predict the difficulties of turning these groups into a finely tuned machine. There is no way that they are a team or will become a team because they lack interdependency. The accounts payable clerks operate in physical and functional isolation from the professionally trained financial analysts. While there is some functional relationship, it tends to be between the supervisors rather than the clerks and analysts. Although it is possible to do team building on the smaller units of the organization, these units must be considered natural work groups, that is, people who work on similar activities, but operate independently of each other.

Characteristics of Natural Work Groups

Natural work groups:

- Have functional relationships, but not functional interdependencies.
- Have common overall higher level goals, but separate and distinct activities.
- Have a common manager, but usually subgroups have different relationships with that leader.
- Usually exist for organization chart cleanliness, not for the functional relationship.
- Usually have very distinct skill specialization (e.g., business analysts, payroll clerks, and systems designers).

These parts of the organization can be more or less effective depending on how their needs and outputs are coordinated by the manager. Although groups can be a very efficient way of addressing a wide range of organizational issues, in most cases they do not address the need for effectiveness.

Needs of Natural Work Groups

Natural work groups have several needs to be more effective:

- A common higher level goal/objective. Although each group may play only *one* part in achieving that higher goal, each group needs to have that focus to understand how its contribution fits into the bigger picture.
- A specific lower level goal/objective that describes the group's own specific target. The overall objective is almost never real enough for natural work groups. They have difficulty relating to it because they are outside the mainstream.
- Very clear interface or linkage expectations. Because subunits are not totally independent, conflict usually occurs when they come together or fail to come together.
- Team skills for natural work group subunits. The accounts payable clerks can be developed into a team; the whole finance department cannot.
- Mutual respect and understanding of each subunit's roles and people. In natural work groups, unhealthy competition or professional jealousies can be counterproductive.
- Cross-skilling, which can still be used within the subunits. Across subunits, it can be used only for career development purposes.

Summary

Natural work groups are organizational structures that carry out related but different activities under a common manager. Meetings usually occur between subunit supervisors and the manager. Information is exchanged, but is not necessarily jointly analyzed or discussed. Conflicts are handled by upward delegation to the top of the structure. Managers and supervisors are "link pins." The subunits are a reflection of the subunit leader's style.

NATURAL WORK TEAMS

In this type of structure, the word "groups" has been replaced by the word "teams." Based on our earlier definition of a team, this means that the key element of interdependency has replaced mere relationships. This form of organizational structure is characterized by a common set of goals and segmented work activities that lead to a specific set of results. Members' activities are both independent and interdependent and are coordinated by a team leader or supervisor. These teams can be considered a loosely held-together collection of individuals. On a daily basis, they tolerate the roles of others, and only under stress do they work together in an optimal fashion. In refineries and chemical plants, it is common to see shift teams that constantly battle maintenance and lab people. However, during a unit shutdown for a planned refurbishing of the unit, everyone seems to cooperate at a level that is amazingly out of character.

The primary focus for natural work teams is the creation of a product or service. People are organized to fit into the technical requirements of getting the work done. Because they are organized around the work, it is not unusual to see wastage and conflict in the human relationship component. The interdependencies are not built into the work, but rather are managed as and when required. The following example illustrates this concept. (Although we use a chemical plant to explain the concept, other examples include assembly teams in a manufacturing plant, system support teams in a data center, or a government social services office.)

Organizationally, the shift team for our example chemical plant is organized as follows (see Figure 4.2):

- Shift teams of process operators (eight to ten) plus one supervisor
- Centralized maintenance (nine people to cover all trades) plus one supervisor
- Centralized lab unit (four to six people) plus one supervisor
- Dispatch/Receiving (four to six people) plus one supervisor.

The process shift team operates the equipment to convert raw material into finished product. Although they work together as a team, team members change frequently, based on shift

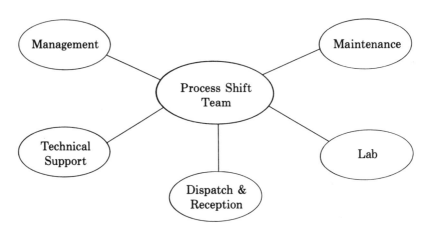

FIGURE 4.2 NATURAL WORK TEAMS

schedules. The operating belief is that a trained operator is required to do a particular job, and as long as each post is covered, the job will get done. The team cannot do its job without the necessary interaction of lab, maintenance, dispatch, and receiving and technical units. However, these people are not part of the team and all necessary interactions occur only as and when required. The obvious difficulties happen when the process teams have to wait for a lab test to be done, a maintenance person to show up and fix something, or a dispatch person to finish loading or return from a break.

Overtime is a constant cost of doing business in this form of organization. Cooperation between shift-team members and support units depends entirely on the interpersonal skills of the appropriate supervisors.

Characteristics of Natural Work Teams

Natural work teams have a number of common features:

- Members have functional interdependence on each other and with other parts of the organization.
- There is a common area of responsibility, but different subactivities support it (e.g., an outside lab).
- A common leader is established (e.g., plant manager).
- Conflicts are resolved between supervisors.
- The structure is driven by a common goal, not the organizational chart.
- Different skills exist on the shift team, but some overlap occurs (e.g., several members can usually run the control board).
- Seniority usually dictates who gets what job on the team.

Needs of Natural Work Teams

Natural work teams have several needs to be more effective:

- All members and supporting units need a common long-term goal.
- Working relationships have to be clear and negotiated between supervisors.
- Some cross-skilling can be implemented to reduce downtime and wastage.
- The core team needs good communication skills and documentation skills because team members change frequently.
- The core team supervisor is a critical information source and coordinator.

Expectations for Natural Work Teams

It is reasonable to expect the following of a natural work team:

- Present performance standards (i.e., quantity and quality) are *usually* met. Exceptions will occur and are managed by supervisors and managers. The team does not accept responsibility because key support variables are outside their control.
- Progression for people is seniority based, and transfers are usually to other units in the plant. Growth is not expected for members on the team.
- Loyalty to the team is not expected because membership is a function of shift scheduling.
- Continuous improvement activities must be driven by the supervisor with different levels of involvement from

team members depending on personality, availability, and willingness.

- Individuals are responsible for their own actions and behaviors. Members are not expected to accept responsibility for other team members or the team as a whole.
- Teams will follow prescribed procedures and will meet the performance expectations, if supervisors can manage the interfaces between support units effectively.

Summary

Natural work teams are a form of organization that allocates people to prescribed jobs and ensures that the support functions exist to help them. Interdependencies exist and influence the ultimate success of the team. The supervisor (team leader) is critical to the success of natural work teams because of the changing team makeup and the need to manage linkages of information and support functions. Natural work teams are effective in meeting clearly prescribed performance goals. They are frequently used to obtain guaranteed minimal performance.

INTEGRATED TEAMS

Integrated teams are also known as intact or cohesive teams. We use "integrated," which seems to us to be a better description of the concept of being together and accepting team responsibility. Integrated teams are the product of a planned organizational shift in philosophy. They have to be consciously created and molded through training and job redesign. In integrated teams, the work is designed to fit key elements:

- Customer requirements
- Business objectives or goals
- Technical operating requirements (i.e., what is inherent in getting all the work done)
- Social requirements (i.e., the best way of meeting team member needs).

On an integrated team, the same people work together on an ongoing basis. If shift work is involved, the team members rotate shifts as full teams, not as individuals. The concept of integrated teams is more than simply togetherness. It assumes an acceptance of responsibility for the work to be done and the behavior of the team. Unlike a natural work team, responsibility is not left to the supervisor. In fact, the supervisor is more of a team leader, team coordinator, or team facilitator.

For such a team to exist, the nature of how work gets done must be addressed. This is the role of job redesign. Traditional organizational structures (i.e. natural work groups and teams) have far too many control features to permit individuals and teams to exercise empowerment. Integrated teams can work in only two situations:

1. A start-up operation that designs jobs to operate in an empowered mode

2. A redesign of current work/control practices to remove the barriers that would inhibit integrated teams.

To illustrate the concept of an integrated team, it might be useful to describe what would happen if the chemical plant used previously to illustrate the concept of a natural work team were to convert to an integrated team. As shown in Figure 4.2, the natural work team components function rather independently. Figure 4.3 shows how the components would function as an integrated team. This diagram represents a very different set of assumptions regarding how the work can get done. The integrated team assumes total responsibility for the production of the product, including:

- Receipt, testing, and storage of raw product
- Processing of raw material, including the responsibility for collecting statistical process control data and managing process parameters
- Carrying out those maintenance activities that are ongoing and within the skill level of the team (e.g., changing filters)
- Lab testing, which is done by all members of the team
- Management of ongoing team issues (i.e., performance reviews, performance management of individuals, purchasing, etc.)
- Sufficient cross-training of team members to carry out functions previously allocated to specialist support groups, reducing dependency on external groups

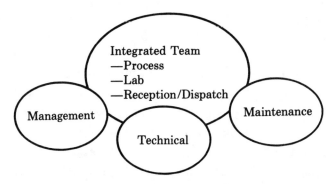

FIGURE 4.3 INTEGRATED WORK TEAM

- A modified wage system that pays for knowledge and skills
- Access to information to make operating decisions (e.g., customer information, cost data and planning information) and the authority to make those decisions.

Characteristics of Integrated Teams

Integrated teams are characterized by a combination of attributes:

- Functional interdependence—Each team member interacts with all other team members and depends on their performance to create an end product that meets customer requirements.
- Job redesign—Work is redesigned to reflect the optimal way to get work done.
- Performance management—Team members accept responsibility for their own performance and the performance of all team members.
- Cross-skilling—Team members are trained to perform a wide range of jobs. Each team member retains a specialty; however, this is supplemented by skill development in other areas. The degree of development of other skills depends on operating needs, not on personal wants.
- Payment for knowledge and skills—Perhaps the most contentious issue involves the necessary change to the reward system. The base rate of pay reflects the learning and application of skills, not specialization and seniority.
- Cohesive shifts—To ensure the ability of teams to operate as an integrated team, it is necessary to schedule these

teams as cohesive shifts. This simply means that the same people are always scheduled to work together.

- Job rotation—For cross-skilling to occur, a planned rotation of tasks must be built into the system. People are assigned by the team to work different jobs as part of the work schedule.

- Team leadership—Integrated teams do not mean self-directed teams. Although a team may evolve into a self-directed team, during the first several years, a team leader or coordinator (often the former shift supervisor) serves a coordinating and facilitating role. The massive training requirements involved in the transition toward integrated teams requires full-time coordination.

- Continuous improvement—An integrated team creates a requirement for constant change. Because work is designed around people, there is an ongoing state of opportunity to change and modify work procedures. Integrated teams require a high level of tolerance for change and an acceptance of responsibility to make things better.

- Empowerment—The above characteristics are worthwhile only if empowerment is included as a fundamental principle. Integrated teams are clearly empowered to decide on a wide range of operational issues. Without empowerment, the other characteristics prove to be a waste of energy and valuable resources.

Summary

Although integrated teams are an option for organizations seeking a truly participative management philosophy, many organizations can increase participation and involvement without the severe changes required for integrated teams. Tremendous improvement can occur by increasing the effectiveness of natural work groups and natural work teams.

Before going to the extreme of integrated teams, the senior manager must answer "yes" to the following questions:

1. Am I willing to allow the redesign of work practices by a redesign team populated largely by the people who do the work?

2. Am I willing to change my reward system to pay for knowledge and skills?

3. Am I willing to absorb the up-front cost required to cross-train workers?

4. Am I willing to empower teams to make decisions about those issues that affect them?

5. Am I willing to champion a strategy that will be resisted by many managers and workers?

6. Am I willing to create and live in an environment of open and honest communication?

7. Am I willing to be judged by my actions rather than my words?

8. Am I willing to share decision making with the union or employee representatives?

9. Am I willing to live through the three- to five-year transition period that will appear to be less effective than traditional strategies?

10. Am I willing to be a leader?

Finally, that manager needs to consider another question: What's the payoff if I answer yes to these ten questions?

SHORT-TERM TASK/PROJECT TEAMS

A fourth option for organizations is the use of parallel task teams. By "parallel," we mean existing in partnership with the chosen organizational chart/structure. The three previous options focused on how to organize people around the cross-functional issues that need to be resolved without changing the organizational chart. The purposes of task teams are consistent with the purposes of the three previous options; however, they tend to be more limited in nature. Several typical purposes are:

- To increase participation of people on specific issues
- To ensure a wider range of input from people who are affected by an issue, but who do not work together in its day-to-day resolution
- To resolve a "single-time, nonrecurring issue" with maximum input without adversely affecting the ability to meet core business goals
- To resolve issues that are beyond the empowerment of individuals/teams to ensure the avoidance of isolationism.

Task teams can be used effectively to increase the participation of employees in an organization. Many companies have intentionally used quality circles, improvement teams, and other forms of problem-solving task forces to cross organizational boundaries on specific issues. Clients that are using this approach include Bell Canada, Xerox, General Electric Canada, General Motors, and Martin Marietta.

One benefit of this strategy is the minimal disruption to existing work practices and organizational structure. Many organizations that are undergoing a total culture change, including work redesign, will frequently use project teams as a complementary strategy to deal with cross-functional issues.

There are basically two types of project teams, specific issue/task teams and improvement teams. These are discussed in the following sections.

Specific Issue/Task Teams

The driving force behind the creation of a specific issue/task team has been preidentified by someone in the organization with enough authority to create such a task force. Characteristics of a specific issue/task team include:

- The team has a preidentified issue or task.
- The team usually has cross-functional purposes.
- Team members are usually nominated by the "home" organization. Involvement might be voluntary within that organization.
- Specific time frame exists to achieve goals; then the team is disbanded.
- Leadership is rarely negotiable.
- The mandate usually includes recommendations, not decisions.
- Team members usually have a dual role of representing others and being a team member of the task force.
- The assignment usually is not full time.

Needs of Specific Issue/Task Teams

Because of the artificiality of this form of structure, some very specific needs exist that must be addressed if they are to be successful. Although many of these needs are similar to those of other teams/groups, they have a special impact on specific issue/task teams.

- Goal clarity—Because of the temporary nature of task teams, the mandate must be identified early and revisited constantly. Because people focus on their prime job, for which they get paid, it is normal for the task team goal not to be paramount in their thoughts. Also, because of the dual role of team member and constituency representation, there is frequently potential for conflict in the team. The team needs clarity as to whether the goal is to redesign work practices, or to effectively represent the "pipe fitters" in the redesign effort.

- Role clarification—People usually work out the "pecking order" in their day-to-day jobs. Task teams create a new and potentially threatening situation to team members. Members need to spend time clarifying the expectations they have of themselves, the other team members, and the team as a whole. If the team member is representing a function or constituency in the organization, it is critical that he or she have a clear mandate from his or her own organization.

- Group process—Because task teams meet infrequently, these teams must have a clearly defined and agreed upon process for addressing issues and behaviors. Each team member comes to the meetings with different approaches to solving problems, resolving conflict, and reaching consensus. The task team cannot be successful unless it confronts the need to establish its own set of behavior norms and decision-making procedures.

- Performance management—Normally, each team member is nominated or invited to the task team as a representative of a part of the organization or because he or she possesses skills or knowledge critical to the team's success. Once the members become part of the task team, a portion of their performance moves away from the supervisor or manager who normally has responsibility for evaluating their performance. The project team leader does not have a mandate to develop the resources or skills of the team member. This gap of performance management responsibility can create some problems. For example, the team member may "float" and not contribute to the best of his or her abilities. Alternatively, the team member may work hard, accept responsibility, and contribute much more than others. In either case, the team member may think that no one at the "home" organization will ever know about his or her team behavior. For these reasons, task teams need to ensure that the performance of team members gets communicated to those people ultimately responsible for the members' growth and development.

HAZOP Team Example

The Esso Chemical's Hazardous Operations (HAZOP) team represents an effective use of short-term task teams as a means of increasing involvement and meeting business goals. In the petrochemical industry, organizations perform hazard identification and risk analyses on an ongoing basis. Every new change in equipment and procedure is subjected to a full impact analysis for risks and hazards prior to implementation. Supplemental to this ongoing analysis, every three to five years a full plant HAZOP analysis is conducted by the safety coordinator and plant engineers to ensure that incremental changes have not affected the overall safety and environmental levels of the plant.

In 1990, Esso Chemicals was due for its full HAZOP analysis. In line with the new philosophy of participative management, the organization decided to approach this project in a totally different manner. Three task teams, which were formed to conduct the plantwide HAZOP analysis. The teams which were composed of operators, maintenance workers, supervisors, and managers, were led by project team leaders who were engineers. The philosophy was that the people closest to the work were the best informed to carry out the task.

Recognizing the needs of the members of the HAZOP teams, the maintenance manager arranged for a series of team-building workshops to ensure that team members had the tools to be successful. Some of the results of those workshops are listed below to illustrate how task teams need to organize their activities.

HAZOP Mission

- To control risks by the management of change process supported by the skills of process–mechanical–technical teams.
- To evolve to a true quality process in the control of risks, including the inherent continuous improvement and self-monitoring of progress.
- To achieve future risk analysis that focuses on ways to control risk, deemphasizing HAZOP on existing facilities.

Long-Term Goal of HAZOP Teams

- To have completed a HAZOP risk analysis and recommended improvements by 31 October 1991.

Short-Term Goal

- To have developed action plans for conducting HAZOP by the end of the workshop.

Immediate Goal

- To establish HAZOP team goals, roles, structures, and procedures to identify a starting point by the end of day one.

Roles   The team determined that it needed to identify the following structural roles:

- Project team leader—This role was preassigned, but clarifying what leadership meant to this team had to be resolved.
- Meeting chairperson—The team defined a need for a chairperson. The role of the team leader was not seen as necessarily the role of the chairperson. The role of chairperson was to rotate on a voluntary basis. The chairperson was responsible for the agenda.
- Scribe/facilitator—This role was to rotate on a voluntary basis and was to keep discussion and agenda items on track.

The team also needed to identify the following informational roles:

- Information sources—The team decided that all team members had a role in providing the raw data about operational activities in the HAZOP review.

- Information analysis—The team decided that all team members had a role in assessing and judging data to develop recommendations. Specifically, the team would not allow a team member to represent his or her own function without accepting responsibility to help develop plantwide solutions.
- Decision maker—The project team recognized that their role was to make recommendations. Ultimate decision-making responsibility remained with the business manager.
- Group roles—Based on an analysis of their preferred style of operating in groups, the following roles were identified: clarifier, summarizer, challenger, facilitator, champion, and sponsor.

Group Process   The task team then discussed the procedures they would use in discussing the data and developing recommendations:

- Administrative/task team decisions (i.e., timing/frequency of meetings, etc.) were to be made by majority vote.
- Procedural decisions (i.e., how to get started, plan of attack, etc.) were to be made by consensus.
- Task team recommendations (i.e., the output of the team) were to be made by consensus.

Summary   The HAZOP team is a classic example of a task team. The specific time frame (a year) and the cross-functional membership are common features of a task team. Within Esso, the HAZOP teams are still completing their assigned duties. Results are not yet available on the relative success of these teams compared with more traditional responses.

However, the conceptual framework indicates that the quality of their analysis should be greater, and the ownership of responsibility more widespread.

Improvement Teams

A second type of project team is the improvement team. These teams became fashionable in the quality-circle approach to participative management. They can be very successful as a short-term strategy to increase people's involvement. However, as a total strategy, they fail to address some key issues within an organizational culture, including:

- Reporting relationships
- Reward systems
- Information flow
- Empowerment.

These issues are not necessarily affected by improvement teams.

Characteristics of Improvement Teams

Improvement teams:

- Can be cross-functional or within a department
- Are usually voluntary
- Are usually not a full-time activity
- Usually have a life expectancy
- Are usually responsible for problem identification, priority setting, and recommendation

- Are rarely empowered (Martin Marietta is an exception)
- Usually focus on problems within work sphere of group members
- Are usually led by outside facilitator

Additional characteristics of improvement teams are the following:

- Members can change/rotate.
- A group process is usually dictated by the facilitator.
- The group thrives on motivation and enthusiasm. Conflict and long-term working relationships are not addressed.
- The team has a high impact on the obvious problems. Such a team is harder to use on long, drawn-out problems. The group needs to see success early to be effective.

Improvement teams are a high-payoff strategy in the short term. They should be seen as a means of quickly demonstrating the power of involving workers. However, experience seems to show that if nothing else changes in the work environment, there is a decrease in the payoff.

General Electric's Work-Out Process

General Electric (GE) has one of the most successful implementations of improvement teams we have seen. Several factors led to the success of their process, known as "Work-Out." These factors include:

- Support from the top of the corporation—GE Chairman Jack Welch has created a vision: "We can create an environment where every man and woman in the company can see and feel a connection between what he or she does all day . . . and winning in the marketplace . . . the ultimate job security."

- Driven by business objectives—People are getting involved to increase organizational effectiveness. In the words of Steve Snyder, president of CAMCO, GE Canada's major appliance subsidiary, "Participative management is a business decision."

- Full implementation—Over 10,000 employees in GE Canada (and over 300,000 GE employees worldwide) will participate in "Work-Out" sessions by the end of 1991.

- A Work-Out session usually runs 2½ days and brings together employees from all levels and functions, including senior management.

- Local top management involvement—It is not enough to have a video of the chairman discussing his vision. People know it's important when their "bosses" show up.

- Speed of approval—Over 70 percent of small group recommendations are approved on the spot by the local management team.

- Recognition—GE reports constantly through its internal newsletters. People are recognized for their contributions with glowing write-ups and pictures.

- Continuity—GE plans to continue "Work-Out" sessions as part of an ongoing business plan. It is not a "one-off" program.

Although other factors contribute to improvement of team effectiveness, these stand out as some of the most significant.

Summary

Improvement teams function parallel to the existing organization's structure. They are particularly effective when used cross-functionally. People become aware of the relationships between their jobs and the many other people who affect their jobs in some way, but whom they might not normally meet in the course of day-to-day business. We totally support the use of improvement teams, but only as part of a more integrated strategy of increasing participation.

LONG-TERM COMMITTEES

A new word now appears in our classification of parallel organization structures—"committee." Specifically, we are addressing committees that exist on an ongoing basis in the organization. Short-term committees, such as holiday party and summer picnic committees, are actually task forces with glorified titles. Most committees are created to meet some cross-functional and ongoing need. They generally meet monthly and address issues that relate to the need to create consistency across the organization. Several examples of long-term committees include plant safety committees, environmental committees, and salary and benefits committees.

For the purposes of this book, we focus on one specific committee that exists in the strategy of participative management: the steering committee. The role of the steering committee is covered in more detail in Chapter 3; however, a few words here will clarify this commonly used structural approach.

Within the overall strategy of participative management, many organizations create a steering committee. The goals are many and usually include the following:

- Establish boundaries within which teams are empowered
- Champion the strategy of participative management by active support
- Provide resources in terms of dollars and training for teams
- Model the behaviors and activities that teams should be using
- Provide external liaison and negotiations with other stakeholders in the organization, such as corporate offices, other parts of the organization, and external suppliers
- Be a review panel for those recommendations that exceed the empowerment of the teams and that require a significant commitment of resources for implementation
- Facilitate the exchange of information between teams to maximize the learning and minimize the repetition of mistakes.

What makes a steering committee different from other forms of organizational structure is its composition. Politics plays an important role in the formation of steering committees. It is the only forum that requires the active representation of the union or employee representatives. Normally, a steering committee is composed of a chairperson (i.e., the top on-site management person, who serves as the change leader) and the following members:

- Chairperson of plant union or employee representation group
- Each business unit manager
- Several additional union representatives (sometimes all of them)
- Human resources manager.

Martin Marietta in Denver also includes full representation from the customer of the organization, the U.S. Department of Defense, because all projects are funded by this single source.

The makeup of the steering committee is critical because it must establish the vision, strategy, and tactics for participative management. The committee makes decisions. Thus, the members must be at a level that can commit the organization's resources to action. Any team initiatives will disappear if the recommendations cannot be responded to in a timely, decisive manner. Max DePree, chairman of Herman Miller, in his excellent book *Leadership is an Art* (Wiley, 1989), describes leadership as something that is owed to the people in the organization. Similarly, teams are owed a form of leadership in the strategic implementation of participative management. This is the role of the steering committee.

SUMMARY

This chapter attempts to differentiate among different forms/ structures used by organizations. Several summary points are worth repeating:

- There is no one way to structure for increased participation.
- Groups are not less important than teams.
- Teams must be used only when interdependency exists between team members.
- Teams should be formed only after analyzing the organizational work practices and required relationships.
- More than one form of team can be used within an organization.

- Participation and empowerment can increase without sociotechnical redesign and a full conversion to integrated teams.
- Leadership is still critical in teams and groups.
- Teams are not an end in themselves; they are a means to more effective business results.

5

How Teams Work

In Chapter 4, we covered the various types of teams and groups that exist within an organization. In describing the characteristics of those teams and groups, we also addressed some requirements that help those teams be effective. This chapter focuses on basic team processes that are required for a team or group to be effective in achieving its task or goal.

To understand the key elements of team effectiveness, one must understand the process of group activity. Establishing a group is frequently a haphazard activity based on more than the potential interrelationship of its members. People are brought together for many reasons, and there is frequently an expectation that discussion will result in resolution and agreement. This interesting philosophy is totally unsubstantiated. In sports, a newly formed team does not expect to operate anywhere near its peak efficiency. That team expects a breaking-in period before becoming effective. Nevertheless, management expects relative strangers to operate in an efficient and effective manner without prior relationships, experience, or group history. Frequently, this naivete is accompanied by a lack of rules, external arbiters, or agreed commonality of purpose.

Theorists have studied group process for many years. Early work in the National Training Laboratories, by Leland Bradford and others, focused on individual and group behaviors that occurred in working groups. Many advances were made on the data generated by these theorists. Most of these theorists focused on the group. In their studies, the group seemed to exist independently of the purpose or task that created it. The result was an escalation of individual behavior analysis and a decrease in the concern about team or task effectiveness.

As we become more involved in attempting to increase team effectiveness within our client organizations, this narrow focus on the individual seemed less practical in achieving the desired levels of team effectiveness. About this time, we came across what we considered to be a fairly significant approach aimed more in the direction in which we were progressing. This work, developed by Mark Plovnick and Ronald Fry, is called task-oriented team development. They suggested that the group should focus on clarifying the task, the members' roles, the procedures and processes, and the relationship and individual-behavior components of teams. They contended that if members did not have a clear understanding of why they were there, what the team was to do, and how members were to interact and be successful, the result would be relationships characterized by many behavioral or individual problems. Plovnick and Fry felt that these problems would be avoided by taking a more structural approach to teams.

Based on our experience, we have modified Plovnick and Fry's approach to represent a model of team effectiveness we believe is essential for any team or group. We recognize that it is presumptuous to indicate there is a single prescriptive solution for any team or group. Because every group and team is different, slight variations will be required in the application of this model to each group.

TEAM EFFECTIVENESS MODEL

The following is a simplified version of the model we use in working with client organizations. This simple four-stage questioning process should be followed to some degree to guarantee effective performance of groups and teams.

1. *Goals.* Why are we here?

2. *Roles.* Why me? Why everybody else? What is expected of me, and what do I expect of others? What do I bring to the group?

3. *Processes.* How are we going to handle the process of achieving the goal? How will we work together to make decisions, resolve conflicts, and so forth?

4. *Relationships.* How are we going to handle ourselves and our interactions to achieve the goal? Who's who on this team, and what does that mean for our working together?

The simplicity of this four-stage model seems to imply a degree of oversimplification of the complexities that normally occur within teams. Each step needs to be explained more fully to indicate how each contributes to team effectiveness and to identify the degree of difficulty that occurs in each step.

GOAL CLARIFICATION

The first step of any established group is to clarify the reason for its existence. It is impossible to operate effectively if no clear, agreed upon purpose is driving the team and its members. It must be the first issue dealt with because all the team's activities are aimed at achieving the goal. Without understanding the goal, the remaining steps in the model become undirected and meaningless. Frequently, we find it useful in the goal-clarification process to establish three levels of goals:

1. The long-term goals
2. The short-term goals
3. The immediate goals.

Long-Term Goals

Teams must understand their long-term mission or purpose. Frequently, this goal is imposed on the team. It often is tied to a vision or mission statement that is larger than the team itself. Because it is imposed does not mean it does not have to be discussed, clarified, and agreed to. An imposed goal that has not been accepted is worse than no goal at all. A long-term goal is usually to be achieved within one to five years in the future, and it represents a vision of the preferred future under which this team will be operating at the end of that time.

Long-term goals provide a strategic direction that lets team members know where they are going. A long-term goal, such as "To be a world-class supplier of Product X by 1993," may be important for looking into the future; however, it does very little to affect people's day-to-day performance. Teams have great difficulty staying excited about their work and understanding what they should do every day if they are given only the long-term goal. Thus, we have found it necessary to help teams develop short-term goals, which impact their ongoing activity more than the long-term goals.

Short-Term Goals

A long-term goal without an identified progress point becomes useless. A long-term goal is directional and is rarely easily measurable. Short-term goals are specific, measurable points the team must set to mark whether they are making progress toward the long-term goal. Some examples of short-term goals would be:

- To produce X tons of product at 95-percent prime quality by December 1992.
- To have all manufacturing processes in statistical control by 1992.
- To implement a reliability program by December 1991.

In looking at these short-term goals in relation to the long-term goal, it is apparent that all the short-term goals can be measured and can be specifically actioned by the team members. Short-term goals can range from three months to one year, depending on the complexity of the task facing the team. They can be built into overall work plans, and day-to-day and week-to-week planning activities. Yet these goals do not exist in a vacuum. There has to be a relationship between the company's short- and long-term goals, because the short-term goals are a means to achieving the long-term goal.

Immediate Goals

Establishing immediate goals is in our view the most important of the goal-clarification activities undertaken by teams. Our experience has shown us that although short-term goals are meaningful to teams, without more immediate goals, the teams experience a great deal of frustration during meetings. A frequent comment we hear from team members is, "I am not against teams, but I am against all those stupid meetings where we never seem to get anything done." To avoid this sense of frustration, the team needs to establish clear goals for each meeting.

Immediate goals represent the specific objective for each meeting as it occurs. People need the reinforcement that comes from achieving goals. Because short-term goals may not be achieved for three months to a year, it is hard to maintain the team's motivation without getting some feedback about progress. The function of immediate goals is to ensure that the team continues to have a feeling of success. They can point to a specific achievement following a meeting on an issue. Some examples of immediate goals for teams are:

- Deciding on appropriate charts to use for gathering statistics
- Developing a reliability maintenance system for the plant
- Identifying reliability activities, by priority, for the next three months (i.e., what equipment gets attention first, second, third, etc.).

Although it may sound as though we are complicating the issue of long-term, short-term, and immediate goals, it is critical to remember that although the long-term goal, once it is established, usually to be achieved in one to five years, it needs to be revisited but not thoroughly discussed at every meeting. Similarly, short-term goals frequently need to be referred to but, once established and agreed to by the team, do not have to be the subject of discussion at every meeting. The immediate goals, however, must be reestablished at every team meeting so the members have a clear understanding of each meeting's purpose. Thus, only the immediate goals need to be continually reworked, established, measured, and used as the basis of team effectiveness.

The Appendix includes examples of teams that have produced long-term, short-term, and immediate goals. These are meant to be taken not as perfect statements, but rather as examples of what some teams have found useful to keep them on track.

ROLE CLARIFICATION

Every member of a team is faced with fundamental questions: Why am I here? What do people expect of me? What can I expect from the other members of my team? Without a clear understanding of the answers to these questions, it is difficult for teams to be effective. Every team member (leader included) must be absolutely clear as to his or her role in the group. A lack of role clarity causes a variety of reactions:

1. Frustration, which can be manifested in both mental and physical departures of team members. People simply leave the team.

2. Passive acceptance of the role confusion, which usually causes these team members to be uninvolved and withdrawn. People who were expected to be contributing data to sit back and simply act as receivers.

3. Clarification action, which effective group members attempt to put aside the group task or decision until their role is clarified. To many members of the group, this appears to be dysfunctional behavior, but that is not the intent.

4. Reveling in role confusion, in which people play roles they were not intended to play. This person thinks, "If you do

not tell me what role you want me to play, you have given me the freedom to play any role that I decide to play." This behavior causes problems because confrontation can occur about the validity of the assumed role. For example, a person with certain information about the implications of proposed options and alternatives might be invited to act as an information source for a decision-making group. As the group progresses, that person might become overinvolved in the decision-making process.

Within any team, a range of different roles can and must be undertaken by individual group members. The following roles are not meant to be universal in every team, but they are some of the more common roles that we have seen people trying to identify in terms of increasing a team's effectiveness.

Structural Roles

The first set of roles that need to be clarified are those that have to do with the group structure. These usually include such roles as:

- Chairperson
- Facilitator
- Scribe
- Leader
- Timekeeper.

All these roles represent specific functions that might be performed by any team member. These roles must be clarified to ensure that:

- Effort is not duplicated (i.e., that eight people see themselves as timekeepers and nobody gets involved in the discussion)
- A particular role that is critical to the success of the team is not missed while everyone assumes that someone else is doing it.

In many of the very effective teams we have observed, it is quite common for many of these roles to be rotated.

It is not essential to have all these roles identified in every team meeting or activity. We are merely identifying a range of possible structural roles that might apply in certain team activities. The only roles that seem to give some cause for confusion are the chairperson's, leader's, and facilitator's roles.

Chairperson's Role

In simple terms, the chairperson is responsible for ensuring that:

- The meeting takes place
- Members are informed of the meeting time, place, and agenda
- Members have input to the agenda
- The agenda is agreed to by the team.

Leader's Role

The leader's role is frequently identified by responsibility for the agenda item(s). Formal position within the organization may dictate leadership. In some instances, the leader may defer leadership of discussions to the chairperson or facilitator. This frees the leader to participate fully in the discussion, rather than risk being viewed as manipulating the process.

Facilitator's Role

The facilitator focuses on agreed to procedures and processes, guiding the team's discussions. Sometimes he or she leads discussion with questions and keeping the team on track by adhering to the agenda and preestablished group norms.

Decision-Making Roles

Once team members have decided on the structural roles, they need to agree on the role the individual team members will have within the team's decision-making process. The three main decision-making roles that need to be clarified are:

1. Information source
2. Information analyst
3. Decision maker.

Information Source

A team in a decision-making mode often requires certain information to achieve its goal, or reach effective decisions. In these instances, it can be appropriate to identify that certain individuals are to provide that data. For example, a finance manager might be invited to join a group to provide financial facts, or a group member might be commissioned to study machine capabilities and present the relevant findings. The possession of information does not imply an automatic inclusion at the decision-making level of the group. It is not uncommon to have individuals at the team meeting because they possess data that the rest of the team needs to be able to make a decision. If these information sources are not team members, but are there by invitation, it must be made clear that they do not have a voice in the decision and that consensus does not include their agreement.

Information Analyst

This role is very different from the role of information source. Rather than bringing data to the team, the information analyst evaluates, judges, correlates, assesses, and analyzes the data so effective decisions are made. This role has an assumed or attached responsibility for the decision reached, which is not necessarily true for the information source role. The information analyst's role is based on the proven ability to absorb facts, array information, make value judgments, and balance potential risks and returns. Extending this role to all team members who are going to be held accountable for the results of the decision is normal. To be clear, it is not necessary to separate these two roles; it is common to have a group member provide the data and then retreat to an information analyst role as a member of the team. A person can wear two hats.

Decision-Maker

If the team must make a decision, it must be quite clear who in the group has the responsibility for making the ultimate decision or whether the group as a whole shares the responsibility. One of the earliest issues we insist groups address as they begin their deliberations on any issue is whether they are responsible for *recommending* or *deciding*. It is fundamental that the group fully understands the limitations of the results of its deliberation. If the team's role is to recommend to another body or individual for ultimate approval, this does not alter the process by which the group reaches its recommendation, but it reduces the degree of frustration that occurs if they are overruled by an external body. In Chapter 2, we addressed the myth of democratic management versus participative management, but it deserves reinforcement here. The belief that a member who plays a role in the decision automatically has the right to be involved in the final decision is a myth.

Because these roles are not restricted to one per group member, it is important to identify which role is being performed at any point in time. When a team leader says, "Here's an alternative, let's look at it," is he or she:

- A decision maker looking for acceptance?
- An information source simply providing another option to look at?
- Playing a process-facilitator role trying to move the group forward?

Group members should not have to guess their roles. An effective team clarifies the roles before getting involved in deliberations, and no group member should be present without some clear understanding about his or her expected role performance.

Group Roles

A third level of role clarification involves the individual behavioral roles people play as part of being a team member and as part of the personality they bring to the team. One perceived benefit of teams is that diversity leads to strength. Having different people with different personalities, strengths, abilities, and skills should in the long run leads to increased overall team performance. Nevertheless, people's behavioral roles should be managed.

Much has been written about the types of roles people play. Most commonly, behavioral roles are categorized into task roles, group process roles, and dysfunctional roles.

Task Roles

Behaviors that help the group move toward the achievement of its task or goal are called task roles. Examples are:

- Initiating—Presenting solutions or problems to address
- Information seeking—Helping to gather relevant data
- Clarifying—Asking for new data or interpretations
- Elaborating—Providing alternate interpretations
- Information giving—Contributing data for discussion
- Summarizing—Trying to poll and test consensus
- Polling—Trying to get agreement.

All these behaviors involve moving the group toward achieving its task.

Group Process Roles

Group process roles include behaviors that help the group work more effectively. They deal more with the people than the task. These roles include such typical behaviors as:

- Helping the less vocal people have a say in the discussion
- Sharing feelings about how things are going
- Encouraging others by both verbal and nonverbal behaviors
- Working to harmonize and smooth out differences
- Compromising and seeking middle grounds to avoid conflict
- Providing acceptance and agreement to people and issues.

There must be team members who are comfortable performing these roles. These people are not pushy, but they attempt to maintain the integrity of the team and its members rather than have the task dominate.

For team effectiveness, it is critical *not* to try to change the individual personalities of team members. The team should identify the typical behaviors the team members feel most comfortable with, and assess the existence, range, and completeness of the team's coverage of both task and group roles. For example, if a team found that seven of eight members were task oriented and concerned about pushing toward the goal, and only one member tended to perform group process roles to keep the group together, then that one individual would be expected to have difficulty in trying to help the team, particularly if the group had not agreed to the role he or she would play. We did a role analysis of members of a team we worked with to determine the roles with which members felt most comfortable. Four of seven members reported being most comfortable in the role of challenger or devil's advocate. It is not hard to envisage the potential dangers for a team in which everybody plays devil's advocate, and nobody fills task-oriented roles to keep the team moving forward.

Dysfunctional Roles

Not all roles played by team members contribute to the team's effectiveness. These dysfunctional roles represent behaviors that are not concerned with either the achievement of the tasks or the maintenance of the group. Typical dysfunctional roles include:

- Blocking—Interfering with the group's progress by arguing, resisting, and disagreeing beyond reason or by coming back to the same "dead" issue later
- Withdrawing—Staying out of a discussion, daydreaming, doing something else, whispering to others, and so forth
- Digressing—Getting off the subject, leading a discussion in some personally oriented direction, or making a brief statement into a long, nebulous speech
- Seeking recognition—Calling attention to one's self by boasting, asking for sympathy, loud or excessive talking, unusual behavior.

Summary

It is critical to identify the group roles with which team members are comfortable and then attempt to assess whether there is an appropriate balance in the team. This effort helps to ensure that key roles would, at some point, be represented by various team members. It also helps the task-oriented team members understand the need for someone to take what seems to be a disruptive type of role in terms of addressing the group process side rather than the task side of the team. This form of role clarification may seem to be very time-consuming and overly structured; however, once the role issue has been addressed in the early days of team building, it is a simple matter of checking on an ongoing basis whether the roles people are playing are still contributing to the team's effectiveness.

Processes and Procedures

Once the team understands the purpose of its existence, its goals, and the member's roles, it is appropriate to move to the third fundamental element of the team effectiveness model, the issue of processes and procedures. One of the greatest difficulties for teams is to gain members' agreement regarding the structure and methodology or procedures they will use to carry out their discussions toward achieving their task. If a team member disagrees with the way the team is going to address an issue, it will make no difference whether that person agrees with the goal related to that issue. That person will still have trouble being an effective team member. Instead of starting by discussing issues, effective teams spend some time up front discussing and agreeing on how to go about their tasks. Effective team discussion is more than simply "cerebral popcorn." It is very naive to believe that bringing people together and providing a forum for discussion will lead to solid, effective, and committed action. Teams need a structured approach to be effective in resolving the issues facing them.

A wide number of team processes can be used in team building. There are many ways to structure a discussion so the team will be effective. It might be useful to describe a client situation that Lorne became involved with. Because of the nature of this example, we are unable to use the client's name; however, we are sure that many readers can identify similar situations they have encountered in their own organizations.

Case of Process Confusion

In 1980, Lorne was hired by a multinational company to design a problem-solving and decision-making training program. Lorne uncovered the most interesting scenario while in the early stages of establishing the organization's needs.

In the previous three years, one section of the organization had spent over $100,000 training several hundred of its professional staff in a training program called Synectics, a very effective creativity program from Cambridge, Massachusetts. At the same time, a different part of the organization had invested $100,000 in training several hundred of its members in Kepner Tregoe's excellent Problem-Solving and Decision-Making program, from Princeton, New Jersey. The underlying philosophies of these programs are about as diametrically opposed as is possible in the business of problem solving. Synectics trained its participants to be free, to explore, to move off the issue, and to take "excursions." In other words, the further away one gets from the problem, the more likely he or she is to find a creative solution. Any attempt to restrict discussion or judge data was seen as counter-productive and not helpful in the problem-solving discussion. On the other hand, the Kepner Tregoe program teaches participants that good decision making and team behavior is predicated upon rationally and analytically assembling the facts, judging those facts, and not getting trapped in the process of imagination.

Lorne was hired to design a synergizing program that would allow the benefits of each training program (which are significant) to be realized. The people from the two programs attended meetings together, and the result was total chaos because of their fundamental disagreement on how a discussion should be structured. They were unable to talk to each other because of the training they had received.

Although this may seem to be an extreme example, we think it illustrates very clearly that people with different methodologies for approaching tasks are going to have difficulty working together in teams.

Process Techniques

We are not believers in a single process as the best way to handle every situation. In training teams to be effective, we train them to use a wide range of techniques. More specifically, we train them how to identify when each technique is appropriate. Some techniques we frequently use are:

- Brainstorming
- Problem analysis
- Decision making
- Role clarification
- Force-field analysis
- Conflict resolution
- Creative problem solving
- Nominal group techniques.

It is critical that if we deluge a team with different ways to handle issues, we also teach them when to use each. They must know how to do brainstorming, for instance, and how to recognize when it is the right approach to a particular situation.

Decision Methodologies

After the data have been generated, discussed, assessed, and analyzed, the team is ultimately faced with the question, "How are we now going to decide?" The team must make that decision about the nature of required agreement before the discussion begins. There are many ways for teams to reach decisions, including consensus, unanimity, majority vote, imposition, and plop. (These terms were defined in Chapter 2, Myth 8.)

Common Difficulties in Teams

Some of the most common difficulties we see in teams are:

- The assumption that consensus is the *only* way to make decisions.
- Failure to discuss what type of decision making would occur. (The team inevitably reverts to unanimity or majority vote.)
- Failure to poll people to find out whether the decision has already been made.
- Confusion over the meanings of consensus and unanimity.

1. *Believing that all decisions must be made by consensus.* We discussed this issue briefly in Chapter 2, Myth 5. Participative management is by definition a democratic situation. Many authors have indicated that consensus is the ultimate form of decision making. They also claim that one reason for developing teams is to reach consensus. As we have stated, it is quite clear that many decisions do not warrant the time, effort, and energy that consensus requires. Consensus *should* and *must* be restricted to those decisions for which team members must actively support the implementation of the decision. Many team issues are not that significant and could easily be dealt with by a majority vote (e.g., deciding who should be chairperson at the next meeting).

2. *Failing to decide how decisions should be made.* We frequently work with teams that start discussing an issue without deciding how to decide. When the time comes to make the decision, everyone has polarized around the positions. Had they decided initially that a majority vote was going to carry the issue, most people would be willing to live with that decision; however, once people have decided about the important issue, they will not settle for a majority vote. When a person knows that a majority vote is the vehicle for resolution, he or she is less likely to feel distraught over losing the majority vote. However, if that person thought the team would be going for consensus and somebody later imposes a majority vote, it appears as if somebody is manipulating the team to achieve his or her own purposes. The frustration we see around this issue is constant and is easily avoided with an early discussion of what it would take to resolve the issue.

3. *Failing to poll and assess the degree of agreement.* In an attempt to be democratic and fair, a team that has already reached consensus over an issue might continue to discuss the issue. No one has the initiative to say, "Hey, do we have agreement on this issue? It sounds to me as if we are all saying the same thing." One of the greatest frustrations as a consultant is seeing groups overwork an issue, all in the name of fairness and democracy, when it could have been resolved much earlier. Facilitators frequently take quick polling checks of where the team is and whether team members already agree. This helps groups recognize when they have reached agreement, rather than assuming that people may not have changed their minds because of the discussion.

4. *Confusing unanimity and consensus.* Consensus is defined as the process by which a group agrees to a course of action. All members of the group are willing and agree to support

the implementation of the decision. It does not mean that they necessarily have to agree with that decision. Unanimity is 100-percent agreement. Consensus can be as low as forty percent. Forty percent of the people agree with it but the other sixty percent don't see it as being that significant and don't see any problem in making it work. They would prefer to go a different direction, but it is not a big enough issue in their mind to continue to fight for an alternate solution.

We frequently see meetings degenerate when some people state, "I can go along with that," and others are unwilling to accept and push for people to say "I agree." They confuse the need to agree with consensus.

Establish Group Norms

The final component of processes and procedures concerns the behavioral side of the processes that will be used for team effectiveness. These are known as group norms. Just as a team needs to agree on how to handle data, they must also agree on how to handle behaviors. The team establishes these group norms by agreeing upon guidelines for behavior that will increase the effectiveness of the group. This agreement can be either conscious or unconscious. Somehow the group must generate the limits of acceptable behavior for group members. This can be done through a formal discussion and visible ground rules or through a series of consequences that tend to either reinforce or extinguish certain behaviors.

There are no universal norms that can be transferred from group to group. Acceptable behavior in one group may not be acceptable in another. For example, in a sales meeting between a regional manager and his team of five salespeople, there might be a tacit agreement that it is permissible to accept telephone calls in meetings. In a different group, this would never be tolerated. In some groups, it is acceptable for a member to withdraw and doodle, whereas this behavior would generate conflict and accusations in other groups.

Group norms are important to groups. It is imperative that group members understand norms so they can contribute to the task. When a new person joins an established group, the most difficult problem can be trying to fit in with the unspoken group norms. For example, a leader might welcome a new member and encourage frank, open and candid feedback on any issue. Although each veteran team member knows this would in reality be fatal, the new member could easily believe the words and become the victim of an unwritten group norm.

An effective group consciously develops a set of norms that allows it to manage itself while achieving its task. Members have an understanding of what behavior is permissible. They know what will be perceived as dysfunctional and can modify their own behaviors accordingly.

In managing the decision process, groups must consciously and constantly identify group norms and changes that occur in these norms. Typically these norms can range over a wide area, including:

- Dress
- Seating arrangements
- Location of meetings
- Timing of meetings
- Openness of information sharing
- Conflict creation
- Conflict resolution
- Leadership style

- Group member behavior
- Disruptions
- Quality and quantity of data.

There are two schools of thought regarding the use of group norms. One belief is that group members should take a significant amount of time, before beginning team development, to identify the group norms they think will be important in the management of their affairs. The other belief is that a limited number of norms should be established, but on an ongoing basis. The team should identify those disruptive behaviors that are creating problems in the group, and the norm list should be amended to reflect the significant behaviors.

Of the two schools of thought, we are biased toward the latter. Several job redesign teams, which were having significant difficulty functioning, have proudly showed us as many as thirty-seven norms they had created to influence the behavior of team members. However, we feel that no individual team member can be responsible for monitoring thirty-seven different behaviors in a group meeting. Also, teams that generate norms in the abstract are often developing wish statements or beliefs rather than norms (e.g., "We will have open, candid communication").

Norms also should be checked periodically to determine their relevance to the team. A classic example occurred with a colleague, Monte Christie, who was working with a team that felt a potential problem would occur in the area of individual attack. Thus, a norm created by that team during the first week was, "There will be no personal attacks or ridicule allowed in this team from one team member to another." As the team grew and became more effective and successful, the colleague returned to do some other work with them on team building. The team asked whether they could revisit that norm because they wanted to create a new group norm that stated, "Every team member should be willing to accept personal shots and confrontation." The reason was that they weren't having any fun. They were being so polite to each other that they created an abnormal climate. In their normal workplace, people made funny comments and took shots at people. This group learned that they trusted and respected each other enough to be able to take shots at each other without seriously affecting their relationship. Here was an example of a norm that had to be completely reversed if the group was to be effective.

A team needs to spend some time deciding and discussing how it will operate if it is going to be effective. It should look at how this discussion will be structured, how the decision will be made, and what behaviors will be acceptable within the group as contributing toward the team's success.

RELATIONSHIPS

The individual personalities that make up groups create relationship issues in group situations. In our view, however, the team effectiveness model we have been discussing indicates that if the team's goals, the people's task roles, and the processes and norms are clear, then 95 percent of the potential relationship issues no longer exist. A residual amount of personality conflict can still occur. However, we strongly believe that much of what is dealt with as relationship issues actually reflects the failure to do effective team planning. People's frustrations come out and are seen as relationship issues.

We are not going to spend much time on the issue of relationships. Many excellent psychology and behavioral theory books have been written regarding the behavior and relationship issues of teams. It would be repetitious for us to discuss the topic in detail. Over the years, we have used many effective tools at this stage. One of our favorites is the Myer-Briggs Personality Indicator, which has been very effective to help teams understand and accept different personality types and be aware of the impact individuals have on others. It also increases the understanding of why other people affect you in certain ways. We also have found that personality issues frequently should not be handled as team issues, but rather as individual issues for those team members who tend to be most involved in the relationship issues in the group. Some organizations use such things as the T groups, from National Training Laboratories, to increase people's awareness of their own behavior. In other cases, individual counseling works. A wide range of options exist to deal with the relationship issue.

We believe very strongly that teams can frequently learn how to manage their own effectiveness by establishing goals, roles, and processes. However, the professional outsider is often needed to help teams deal with relationship issues. When personality and psychology become the basis for intervening in team process, we strongly urge the use of professionals. We encourage this not because of our own need to get business, but because we recognize the potential risks involved in not dealing with these issues. Teams are seldom trained to deal with personality issues, and they should not be expected to do so on their own.

6

ISSUES FOR THE INDIVIDUAL

As we stated in Chapter 2, and it bears repeating here, participative management has a traumatic impact on individual managers, supervisors, and employees. In our opinion, too little attention has been paid to the issues that confront individuals when participative management is introduced into an organization. Bob Tannenbaum, a leading expert in the field of change, has expressed concern about the lack of attention the individual receives in the participative management process.* He believes his colleagues may be so enamored with the concept of large systems change that they ignore the impact of those changes on individuals.

In many of today's organizations, the accepted belief is that teams are the building blocks of the organization. Although we agree with this—where it makes sense—a simple extension of this belief is that individuals are the building blocks of teams.

In this chapter, we present a case for proactively paying attention to individuals' needs in the participative management process, rather than waiting for problems to occur and then having to hold up the process while you "fix" the people. We focus first on those issues that are common to all individuals from the perspective of losses and gains. Second, we look at individuality versus team issues. Finally, we focus on some specific issues that are experienced by certain role players in the participative management process.

INDIVIDUAL LOSSES AND GAINS

Individuals experience some losses and some gains in every change process. These losses and gains may be more perceived

* Bob Tannenbaum, January 1990, addressing Pepperdine graduating class of Master of Science, Organization Development, in Palm Springs, California.

than real, but to the individual they feel very real. Theoretically, any change process should result in people feeling they have gained something; however, in reality, this is difficult to accomplish for everyone. Organizations need to strive for individual gains as an objective—it is a key indicator of the success of the change. The following is not intended as an all-inclusive list of individual losses and gains, but it represents those with which we have been involved.

Rewards for Contribution

One leading cause of stress for many individuals in the participative management process is the change in the reward system to be applied. What does a participative management–oriented organization reward, and how do individual contributions get recognized? Most organizations that choose the participative management strategy eventually consider team-based reward systems. This system may lead to the elimination of rewards for heroism by individual "experts." To some people, this can be a demotivator. On the other hand, a team-based reward system does lead to greater equity. There is less of what we call a hero perception (i.e., an individual hero gets rewarded for the efforts of others), and there are more highly motivated groups of individuals. There is also an increased likelihood that more people will increase their contributions, thus creating true synergy for the organization.

Generalization versus Specialization

Individuals fear the loss of their identities in the participative management process. This is closely linked to the previous issue, but it also includes the fact that people have invested a great deal of personal time and effort in becoming the "expert" in their chosen field. Because many participative management systems lean toward more open sharing of knowledge, and they also require broader skills for all employees, this often poses a threat to specialists who believe they will personally become less valued members of the organization. This can lead to a loss of status and a greater loss of role clarity. Traditionally, these roles have been viewed as central to the organization's operating efficiency and have carried great influence, in some cases to the point of being control positions. Participative management reduces this influence significantly.

On the other side of the ledger is the fact that participative management may provide the answers to this dilemma if it is well thought out and planned. Opportunities to develop new roles always exist in participative management organizations. For instance, experts may become consultants to the operating organization. This can increase their sphere of influence to the whole organization. It may require a new set of skills, and certainly requires a different mindset, but we have seen it accomplished very successfully.

The move toward generalization also provides opportunities for organization members at all levels to broaden their knowledge about how their work impacts on the work of others and, more importantly, how it provides new skills to integrate all the work of the organization into higher quality products and services. Problem prevention has replaced fire fighting as the *modus operandi* in every case we have encountered.

The Question of Income

We touched briefly on this issue under rewards for contribution, but here we are talking about issues that sometimes do not surface until the organization is well into implementation. For hourly paid employees in many industries, at least in Canada, overtime and its attendant costs have created a second economy that people have come to require for maintaining or improving their lifestyles. The participative management process may lead to a significant reduction of this income base. If that occurs, then the process may be rejected, or at least actively blocked. Unions will almost certainly demand assurances from management that employees will not lose any income as a result of participative management. Greater and more forceful demands will be put forward on the issue of job security.

Professionals also fear loss of income in the participative management process. Although they do not receive paid overtime in any organizational structure, they are affected because most participative management organizations have fewer managerial positions. For most professionals, this translates into the loss of promotional opportunities, stiffer competition for those that will occur, and the obvious loss of real increased income during their careers.

The compensation issue presents some new and interesting challenges for organizations. It may require a total review and revamping of existing compensation systems. It certainly calls for reshaping the way organizations think about compensation. Fortunately, new systems have evolved over the years that have replaced traditional compensation very successfully and that, when effectively developed, have created a strong support base for participative management. These include profit or gain sharing, pay for knowledge and skill acquisition (versus pay for position), cross-training (another form of pay for skill), unit-based reward systems, and a host of others. New organizational styles and cultures require innovative approaches to reward individuals and groups. If organizations can create new compensation packages for executives (and they do), they should be capable of doing the same for whole organizations. We have found that it is worth the expenditure of resources to explore the options, but very costly to ignore the issue.

Collaboration versus Competition

The statement that "Some people are so accustomed to war that peace might kill them" may be an overexaggeration for describing the kinds of behaviors that go on in organizations, but it is not far off the mark. The point is that individuals know how to compete within their organizations. They have seen role models and have been trained to act like gladiators. They have heard and understood the voices of experience chanting "sink or swim," "dog eat dog," "every man and woman for himself and herself," and "only the strong survive." These statements reflect the rules of everyday living in the organization.

Most individuals, however, do not know how to collaborate. Simply telling people that the game rules have changed, without providing them with the skills to play, results for most people in disequilibrium and a sense of loss. It is frustrating to be informed that you are now expected to be a playmaker but not to score all the points. Skills and knowledge need to be changed for everyone. Rewards and perks need to be redefined. The value of collaborative working relationships needs to be clearly understood and accepted as a more effective approach to creating and delivering quality products and services.

Although competition is not evil, within organizations it can be and sometimes is destructive, inefficient, and wasteful. The time wasted in competing internally is better utilized collaborating to compete together against the external competitors, and thus providing what the customers want and need from the organization. A better expenditure of valued resources is to turn them into positive communities focused on achieving or exceeding the organization's goals.

INDIVIDUALITY VERSUS TEAMS

We believe that teams, provided they have all the knowledge, skill, information, and authority to act, will continually outperform most groups of individual star performers, using any set of performance criteria an organization selects. We have seen it repeatedly, and it has been proven and documented from the often-cited Hawthorne experiments in the 1920s to the quality/productivity teams that permeate Japan, Western Europe, and North America today.

Nevertheless, some individuals vehemently resist the idea of teams. We discussed some of the reasons in the first part of this chapter. In this section, we delve into some other issues we have encountered over the years. We believe these exist in every organization contemplating participative management as an effective process for doing business in the future. The following is our list (in no particular order):

1. *Some people fear that they will lose their individuality by joining a team.* A team may subvert the individuals' needs in order to meet the team's needs or to accomplish some organizational goal. Although people may be required to set aside their personal needs at times for the team to succeed, if this becomes the norm, then the organization needs to examine why this is so, and to make some adjustments to team operating philosophies.

We do not subscribe to the concept of individuals sacrificing who and what they are for the sake of the team. Individuality and teamwork are not mutually exclusive; they should build on each other to create something greater that is additive to both the individual and the team, and therefore to the total organization.

2. *Teams and participative management are viewed by some as techniques to bust unions.* Some managers, particularly in North America, have in fact used, or attempted to use, participative management to eliminate unionization from their organizations. The truth is that unionization is not a cause but an effect of the style of management organizations choose in dealing with their employees. Teamwork may indeed result in eliminating unions from the workplace, but we believe this can occur only when employees feel they can trust management to deal fairly with them on all issues.

3. *Individuals don't want to get stuck on a team with bad actors or poor performers.* This is particularly true in organizations with a history of not resolving these types of problems. Indeed, we know of organizations where everyone agrees not to address behavior or performance problems. In moving to teams, these issues get highlighted very quickly and team members know that unless they are confronted, the team may fail to accomplish its goals and be branded as a poorly performing team. Management may be required to take action on these matters to help the organization move forward in the process, or risk damaging whole teams.

4. *Individuals fool management but not their peers.* This is the flip side of the previous item. Those individuals who have been the poor performers or bad actors fear reprisal from their peers. These individuals know that living and working in a team means that the collective patience of peers may not last long, so they strenuously resist being placed on a team. In

some cases, we have seen these people turn around and become excellent performers with exemplary behavior, thanks to the team and its clarity of expectations and norms. Remember, we said, in some cases; we did not say in all cases. Managers should be prepared to respond if the team requests assistance with a problem individual.

5. *Management is simply trying to brainwash the employees and make them all the same.* This complaint is fairly common in organizations that have been on fad diets. It stems from a belief that if people are in teams, they will conform more easily and perhaps even become "good clones." It is a misguided belief. No two teams are the same, just as no two people are the same. Furthermore, being on a team, in almost every case, makes people less susceptible to any form of "brainwashing" by those outside the team. The team strengthens the individual. That is one reason for having teams.

6. *Some people don't like teams and don't think they are effective.* There are indeed individuals who don't like teams, and for reasons other than those discussed in this book. By and large, we have found these individuals to be loners organizationally. They like their privacy, they like one-on-one competition, they are usually very expert in their line of work, and they believe they can accomplish more on their own than by wasting their efforts collaborating with those who know less than they do. Moreover, they tend to be the people who fared well under traditional management systems and who were highly valued for their expertise. There are options in working with these individuals. If an organization can successfully turn these individuals into team players, they will be invaluable to their teams. If that isn't possible to achieve, the organization may have to find specialist/consultant roles for these individuals, and find creative ways for teams to tap their skills and knowledge.

Clearly, organizations need to explore a variety of options for these individuals, including the possibility of employment in some other part of the larger organization (if that exists) in which participative management and teams are not the accepted way of working. Many organizations undergoing the change to a participative management approach have been successful in accommodating these types of individuals. In the final analysis, however, management must take a position that the organization concepts will not be sacrificed for the sake of any one individual, and that can lead to some difficult decisions, as described in Chapter 2.

7. *Individual accountability becomes a new norm.* In traditional organizations, the individual is accountable to management; in team-based organizations, the individual is accountable to his or her team. That shift is pretty dramatic for many people, and some are not crazy about the idea. Usually, those who in the past escaped scrutiny by overworked managers now come under the scrutiny of their peers. Teams set higher performance standards than most managers. Their expectations of team members are much clearer; they demand greater adherence to team rules; and they are more aggressive in demanding team loyalty. On the other hand, teams tend to take better care of weak individuals; team socialization processes create a stronger sense of belonging and team ownership; and teams practice problem-prevention techniques better than groups of individuals under traditional supervision. We have seen individuals gladly accept the added accountability that teams expect in order to gain the social rewards that accompany it—and some of these individuals had previously been branded as bad actors by management.

This may mean that management has not done its job very well in the past. We think it means something quite different: that teams bring something to the situation that management can't—the understanding of the individual's impact on their dynamics, the understanding of the individual's value to the team, and a different level of understanding of the individual's needs. Another difference we've noticed repeatedly is that teams seem more willing and capable of responding to deviant behavior in ways that resolve the behavior very effectively, once and for all time, and usually without destroying the individual's self-esteem.

OPTING IN/OPTING OUT

How should the team and the organization respond if an individual asks to leave a team? How should the organization and the individual respond if a team decides the individual does not fit? These situations happen, albeit infrequently, and ignoring the situation or forcing the team and the individual to continue to try to work out their issues can be detrimental to both parties. Eventually, the situation will become dysfunctional to the organization and hinder the participative management process.

Individuals cannot opt in and out of the participative management process at their convenience. The organization should build in some methods for ensuring that individuals can resolve these conflicts. The organization can reduce the likelihood of these problems by using a selection process that results in a best fit of compatible team members. It also helps to have the team develop a procedure whereby individuals can move among teams if necessary. The only caution here is not to create a revolving-door process. It is critical that the procedure always encompass the criteria of business operating needs, team skill and knowledge needs, and individual needs. Teams can make sound decisions based on these three criteria.

As far as we know, there are no sound business reasons for anyone to opt out of the participative management process. We view involvement in participative management as part of each employee's psychological contract with the organization. Accepting to work in the organization means accepting participative management as a condition of employment. It has been said that participation is optional until it becomes mandatory. We believe that states the case very succinctly. Although participative management is the antithesis of hard-nosed control management, the organization is not doing it just for the joy of it either.

THE LEADER'S ROLE

If ever there was an argument for having only one individual hero in the organization, this leader's role may be it. Today, more than ever, leadership is one of the hottest topics in North America. It may seem contradictory that an equally hot topic is teamwork; however, we don't see a conflict. To gain teamwork, or any form of participative management, you must have someone in the leadership role who is interested in and capable of creating the necessary environment and culture. We do not intend to rehash everything that has been published about this subject. There is enough already on the bookshelves to wear down even the heartiest of resistors to the concept of leadership. In this section, we address the many issues facing the leader who decides on participative management as a valid strategy for his or her business.

"Change must be led" is an often-stated phrase, implying that without leadership there is no change of any significance. However, taking on the leadership role in participative management is a major long-term challenge for any individual. This role requires a person with very special characteristics, not the least of which is the fortitude to weather many storms and attacks on his or her values, beliefs, and principles. The leader must, in some instances, be willing to take on a "Lone Ranger" role, while at the same time having the skills necessary to help diverse people work together in participative management. Metaphorically, we describe this role as similar to walking a tightrope above a snake pit in the dark.

One of the toughest issues faced by the leader is boundary management, that is, dealing with the external world while maintaining momentum inside the organization. The external world comprises stakeholders who measure success by efficiency of getting things done, and who show impatience with the time it takes to change from traditional to participative management cultures. Those stakeholders often include the leader's superiors and peers, some of whom will almost certainly argue that the old ways were good enough. We recommend that the leader develop a supportive relationship with some "significant others" in the external stakeholder groups. In our experience, this strategy has paid off very well in terms of buying time, and in some cases in turning that group into a major support system for the participative management process.

A closely related issue is the need to manage the business while leading the change. The two tasks are difficult to separate at times, and knowing which is appropriate at any given time is a never-ending point of contention. Doug Reid, site manager of Esso Chemical Canada in Sarnia, puts the issue in perspective: "You have to maintain the concept of 'loose–tight' all the time in leading change, and it's not always clear which is appropriate for any given situation." Leaders need to feel free to explore, improvise, and experiment in order to discover their own unique approach to participative management. On the other hand, there is a clear need to maintain some form of business stability throughout the process.

We define managing as the rational, analytical approach to getting the work of the organization done right. We think of leading as a more creative concept, an affair of the heart that has to do with setting visions, getting people to understand and buy in to the vision, and helping the organization to maintain momentum and focus toward achieving the vision. The ability to maintain business stability while increasing employee participation in business decisions is, in our opinion, an art form that evolves through trial and error. There have been enough documented cases of this evolution, by many authors, that we feel certain this form of leadership "art work" is gaining momentum and is here to stay.

Risk Taking and Leadership

Another issue related to leadership is that of establishing a behavior model for the organization. Risk taking—the willingness to try new approaches that go against commonly accepted rules—is not a concept that people subscribe to easily. Traditional organizations are based on what we call the "clone theory" of behavior. Conforming behavior elicits rewards; deviant behavior can lead ultimately to expulsion—boat rockers need not apply.

Participative management organizations, on the other hand, are characterized by the "please walk on the grass" theory. Risk taking and empowered actions are the norms. Errors are used for learning and growth. Guy Tremblay, polymers manager of Esso Chemical Canada in Sarnia, describes the latter approach: "I want people to come to work every day willing to be fired for being different." Let's be clear that we are not talking about taking risks that might lead to unsafe conditions in a plant. We are talking about people challenging why things are done the way they are and why or how certain decisions get made, and putting forth creative, new ideas that previously would have been ridiculed and discarded.

The leader must be willing to set the example for this type of behavior, again and again. He or she must be prepared to take many risks before anyone else in the organization will show any willingness to venture beyond the stages of observers and critics. How many risk-taking examples must be provided by the leader is not clear to us, but it is more than one! Leaders must "walk their talk" in participative management, or look for an easier strategy to implement.

Support for the Leaders

A central question for the leader is, "Did I choose the right strategy?" and he or she will get a lot of input from various factions on this issue. We think that asking this question regularly can have positive results for the leader, since it almost always strengthens his or her resolve and leads to greater constancy of purpose. The leader also will be required to help others in working through issues of security, losses felt by them, role clarity, and many other issues described in this chapter. That requirement alone places high demands on the leader's time and energy, which can be very taxing.

Where does the leader get help and support in dealing with these pressures? We spoke earlier of building relationships with supportive others in his or her peer group outside the immediate organization, and we strongly reinforce that idea as a stabilizing strategy for any leader. There are also networks being formed across North America, and probably internationally, for managers who lead this form of change. These networks offer excellent opportunities to create external support systems for change leaders in that the meetings also address the issues we have discussed in this section. We also recommend the use of internal and/or external consultants as support systems. They are trained listeners, and because they are (or should be) third parties in the process of change, they can be supportive while maintaining an objective view of the process. The third-party role allows consultants to "speak the unspeakable," ask dumb questions, and offer ideas or views that might otherwise not be offered by those who are more closely involved.

Finally, the leader can consider taking the biggest risk by sharing his or her thoughts and feelings with others inside the organization, and seeking their support in working the issues. We have seen this strategy work very successfully. It pulls people together and creates a critical mass of support for the change process. We have also seen it backfire, as some people view it as a sign of weakness in the leader and work against him or her to defeat participative management. Whether to do this requires a judgment call on the part of the leader, who can best read his or her organization. We suggest that some combination of the alternatives discussed here would be most effective, because no single approach is likely to provide the leader with all the support required to carry out his or her vision.

REPRESENTATION ROLE

It is unwieldy, inefficient, and ineffective to get everyone personally and physically involved in all business decision-making processes. Therefore, it makes sense for teams and groups to select representatives who are responsible for ensuring that team or group opinions and ideas are presented to the rest of the organization. This critical role requires special skills and awareness of the inherent responsibilities and accountability. If teams address this role too lightly, they will soon find that their representative may be presenting only his or her own opinions to the rest of the organization. In organizations with which we have worked, this has caused some difficult problems for teams, and particularly for the individual representative.

The importance of the representative role cannot be over-stressed. It is often the primary interface between teams and with the organization at large. If carried out responsibly, this role is an excellent device for increasing the scope of influence that individuals and teams have on the organization. The direct effects range from better quality decisions at all levels, to significant improvements in operating results. The indirect effects include higher morale of employees as they increase their ability to communicate with the rest of the organization, greater ownership and commitment, more improvement ideas, a higher degree of respect between all levels of the organization, and enhanced trust between management and the employees.

Always interesting to us is how the representation scenario gets played out in many organizations. The tendency for most teams, initially at least, is to select a representative who has strong opinions and doubts about the value of participative management to the employees, but acts responsibly in any role he or she undertakes. These representatives frequently question the leaders' motives in selecting participative management as a strategy. They question whether this is simply another work-harder program aimed at taking from the employees to boost quarterly profits. They also challenge most leadership positions and statements about the change process, and they take a defensive posture against moving too quickly on finalizing any decision that affects their peers. They often appear to be blocking the process and self-concerned in their behavior toward the rest of the organization. We have seen these behaviors change as the representatives become more informed about the participative management process, and as they understand more clearly the potential positive impact on the employees.

The timing of this change, from resistance to active support, varies for each person, but we estimate that it occurs in six months to a year, on average. Many variables affect the timing, but we have determined that the leader's constancy of purpose and the emotional level of experiences (e.g., degree of influence on a major decision) are the two major factors in the process. Success in this issue occurs when these representatives become positive thought leaders within their own teams—and they almost always do.

FIRST-LINE SUPERVISOR'S ROLE

How would you like to be labeled "the meat in the sandwich" (the part that always get devoured), "the stumbling block," "the major barrier to change," or any of a myriad of other phrases usually reserved for those people who are viewed by the organization as a major hindrance in any change process? That generally is the fate of the first-line supervisor in organizations that become involved in the participative management process. What's wrong with this picture? These people were promoted from the ranks because they had something management felt would be of value to the organization. They certainly had to be technically competent or they probably wouldn't be considered for supervision at all. Indeed, some organizations select people for these positions solely on the basis of technical expertise. Additionally, management probably believed these people had the potential to lead, if not control, their subordinates. Given their previous value, how did they so quickly become such a negative force in the organization, and what is it that transformed them from fairly effective supervisors into such pains in the neck?

The answer, in our minds at least, is not as complex or mysterious as it often is made out to be. The process of entering into participative management usually goes something like this:

1. The manager believes, or discovers, that by providing opportunities for workers at the lowest levels of the organization to participate in the management of the business, bottom-line results and employee satisfaction can be increased dramatically.

2. The manager describes his or her intent (or vision) to the employees, and invites them to join in exploring and designing new ways for them to participate in the management of the business.

3. Employees and managers begin to implement new participative management systems together, and to reap the considerable rewards.

4. The manager starts to think, "Those people in supervision don't understand what's happening and start acting like turkeys, screwing everything up."

Far too many organizations ignore the supervisor in the planning, design, and implementation stages of participative management. They then wonder why these people become disgruntled and even resentful about the whole process. We are not stating that the organization consciously ignores the first-line supervisor. Our experience is that in most cases the disregard of the supervisor is unconscious. The experience of managers and employees actually working together to create something new and different is so exhilarating and all encompassing that it leaves some mid-level people behind.

In other cases, participative management has led managers and employees to leap to the unfounded conclusion that first-line supervisors are unnecessary and simply do not fit in the participative management process. This conclusion is almost always an assumption, based on little fact and much wishful thinking. The reality is that participative management cannot succeed if the organization does not change the traditional role of the first-line supervisor from that of directing and controlling to one of coordinating and facilitating. In fact, that transformation process is necessary for every level of manager, not only the first-line supervisor.

The first-line supervisor needs to be treated as a valued link in the participative management process, because he or she is the one person who can truly provide the day-to-day support and leadership to the employees. The reasons are simple enough. The first-line supervisor is located with the work group; is involved most closely with the ongoing operation of the business; probably was promoted from the employee group; and more importantly, has a definite stake in the organization's success. Furthermore, the first-line supervisors we have met have been trying for years, without much success, to get management's attention to many of the very issues that get addressed through participative management.

Just like everyone else in the organization, the first-line supervisor needs to have his or her personal and professional needs met through the participative management process. There have to be opportunities for this individual to grow and develop into an even more valuable asset for the organization. In the past few years, more attention has been given to the plight of the supervisor, most notably by Marvin Weisbord (*Productive Workplaces,* Josey Bass, San Francisco, 1987) in some of his recent works on changing the workplace, and the changing role of supervision. We believe that the first-line supervisor role becomes one of leader, business manager, facilitator, coach, mentor, coordinator of assets and resources, and team builder. That should keep him or her busy doing value-added work. The skills required are significant, but they are attainable and most, if not all, supervisors are capable of learning and applying those skills.

This change has to start with a different set of expectations from managers, based on their vision of the future organization, which has to be communicated face-to-face with all supervisors. Next, managers must be willing to spend a significant amount of time with the supervisory group planning how to implement the new role in concert with the participative management process. As with all other roles, the first-line supervisor role must be seen as evolving with the process.

What if a first-line supervisor cannot learn the new skills, or does not want to assume this new role? Both are distinct possibilities, and indeed we have seen both situations occur in organizations. The instances of a first-line supervisor stating that he or she does not want to take on the new role are very rare (security of employment is a great motivator for most people). However, some supervisors may honestly not be capable of taking on the new role, in which case they and the organization should consider the options for these individuals just as they would for anyone else. There may be some individual contributor roles these people could move into and still maintain their own sense of self-esteem and their value to the organization. In cases we've been associated with, some supervisors who chose to return to an hourly paid position were very successful in helping their teams become more effective. The moves were sanctioned by both the teams and the organization, resulting in a win-win situation and great learning experiences for everyone involved. We believe that through the participative management process, organizations can find new and creative ways to resolve such problematic situations with very positive results.

If it hasn't become clear yet, let us state categorically that we believe there is a role for first-line supervisors in participative management. It is central to the process, and the people in this role require a great deal of attention by management.

Have you ever wondered why we separate managers and supervisors, as if they belonged to two distinct and separate groups? Why not change the title "first-line supervisor" to "first-line manager" and acknowledge the fact that these people are indeed managing the business? What people are called often determines how they are treated in the organization, and the first-line supervisor almost always deserves better treatment than he or she receives. We believe it is necessary to legitimize the first-line supervisor role in participative management, rather than attack and obliterate it. By doing so, we think organizations can increase the likelihood of participative management's success many times over. Making any individual feel valued almost always results in greater commitment and increased contribution. In the case of the first-line supervisor, we have seen some unexpected dividends in the form of increased willingness to champion and lead the participative management process, and that pays off in day-to-day returns for the business.

THE INDIVIDUAL AND STRESS LEVELS

Everybody experiences stress. It's what gets many of us out of bed every morning, ready to meet the challenges of a new day.

Without some stress, we become listless and bored. It keeps up alert and productive, and it forms the basis of motivation. On the other hand, too much stress can have some very dysfunctional and unhealthy effects on individuals. This section about the individual and stress levels in participative management serves as a cautionary message to all those who participate in the process. Take care of yourself, and you increase your ability to take care of business.

In the organizational change profession, we need to be constantly aware of the linkages between the change process and the accompanying stress. Change of any kind causes some form of stress in individuals. Change aimed at moving people from that which they know well (i.e., traditionalism in culture, style, etc.) to a new state they don't know well (i.e., participative management) can create enormous stress on the individuals, and thus on the whole organization.

Participative management, to those organizations that view it as a necessary strategy for long-term survival and growth, is a change in every sense of the word. Change usually occurs in three distinct phases, each bringing a different stress level:

1. *Unfreezing.* The need for change is introduced into the organization, and the type of change (e.g., from traditional to participative management) is identified. Stress levels go up. ("What are they doing to us now? Why us?")

2. *Changing.* The change is more clearly defined, plans are developed, and implementation begins. Stress levels go up higher. ("Geez, I didn't think it was going to be this big, this complex, this demanding, this serious. I don't know if I can handle this.")

3. *Refreezing.* The change becomes institutionalized, and the process of refining or fine tuning participative management starts to occur. Stress levels go down for a while, but may remain in a state of flux for some time as the organization adapts to change as a norm for improvement. ("Another meeting? I wish those consultants would stop asking all those dumb evaluation survey questions.")

We stated at the outset that participative management is a process, not a program. Changing an organization's management processes is akin to changing the products it makes. It causes uncertainty, fear, insecurity, apprehension, excitement—that is, it causes stress. Any change causes us to feel stressful, and we each may react differently to stress. A steady diet of high stress, however, can result in individuals losing focus on the organization's goals. It can impact negatively in individual productivity, and in extreme cases it can lead to unsafe acts by employees. In moving toward participative management, individuals may feel a loss of skill as they unlearn old ways, and develop new habits and behaviors to adapt to new organizational norms. No one in the organization is immune. From the executive to the janitor, stress is often evident during the change to participative management, and studies indicate that stress levels do not differ from one hierarchical level to another. The actual stressors may be different for each individual, but the degree to which each feels the stress appears to be fairly consistent. A human resource manager we know said that changing to participative management "feels like every day is a negotiating meeting." That kept his stress level pretty high for a while since he was accustomed to once-a-year, highly structured negotiating sessions.

We have seen some innovative solutions developed to assist groups and individuals cope with the stress involved with the change to participative management. In one organization, the employees bought an exercise bike and set it up in the control center where everyone has access to it. During each twelve-hour shift, employees add a lot of mileage to its odometer! In another organization, from 9:00 A.M. to 9:15 A.M., employees call a time-out and do group stretch exercises in a hallway. Time-outs are a very useful option for reducing stress on the job, and groups can come up with innovative ways to use them. Stress surveys and stress-reduction programs are also very useful techniques for identifying problems caused by too much stress, and for developing new solutions. Employee assistance programs are in place in many organizations today, and they offer excellent resources. If individuals can move beyond their ego-driven need to be seen as self-sufficient, they can access a wealth of knowledge and skill in these programs.

With the move toward more team-based organizations, we have discovered that in creating openness as a norm, both new and long-standing conflicts have surfaced. These conflicts are very stressful. Teams and individuals don't have the skill, or the willingness in some cases, to resolve them. We have found that conflict-resolution techniques are useful skills to give individuals, although we feel that a training program per se may not be the best approach. We tend to lean toward facilitation or developing an intervention (normally by an objective third party) to fit the specific conflict situation. This has two benefits if done properly: First, it helps resolve the existing conflict, and second, it helps the teams and/or the individuals learn some techniques they can apply for themselves when they are faced with future conflicts.

The reward system also can be used very effectively to reduce stress in the change process. We believe that Ed Lawler is right on the money (no pun intended) in his conclusions that new reward systems are needed to support participative management processes, and that those systems need to be delegated downward in the organization. It has been said that "what you reward gets attended to," and we believe that very strongly. If you want people to move quickly from old behaviors to new ones, and shorten the period of stress, then you have to stop rewarding old behaviors and reward only those behaviors that conform with participative management concepts.

Stress is inevitable. What is important is that organizations and individuals understand that they need not become debilitated or paralyzed by its presence. It can be controlled, and there are methods for doing that and maintaining a healthy level of stress that adds value to the participative management change process. In this area, "when in doubt, ask for help" is an excellent rule of thumb.

SUMMARY

In this chapter, we have focused on the individual in the participative management process and some personal issues with which individuals struggle as they experience the effects of participative management. There is no question that participative management directly affects each person in terms of:

- Felt losses and gains
- Individual versus team needs or wants
- Presentation of individual and group needs to the organization
- The leadership role
- Changing roles for first-line supervisors
- Coping with stress in the change process.

We believe it is important to find new ways to alleviate the potential negative impact of these issues and increase the positive impact by turning these issues into opportunities. Solutions require new paradigms, or models, that can be developed only through exploration and a willingness to keep the door of the collective minds open to new, and sometimes off-the-wall, input from inside and outside the organization's boundaries.

7

THE FINAL CHAPTER: WHERE NEXT?

The title of this chapter is a misnomer. There is no final chapter for participative management. As a process, it is organic. It will continue to change and grow as the people and the issues change. It is the openness of a conclusion that both frightens and excites managers.

Because the book to this point has represented a review of our experiences with participative management, it seems appropriate that the final chapter should project into the future. We do not claim to have psychic power; however, some predictions seem to be reasonable. We believe that the following predictions represent what leaders, workers, and unions should expect in the 1990s.

■ **PREDICTION 1** ■

Participative Management Will Grow in Usage by Organizations

By 1995, organizations that have not consciously increased involvement and empowerment will be the exception, not the oddity they are today. This growth will extend beyond the traditional manufacturing and service-based organizations to include government organizations, educational institutions, and health care facilities.

The Canadian Federal Public Service recently launched a program called PS 2000, establishing a vision of how the public service should operate by the year 2000. Their vision statement reflects a diametric change from current practices:

"An Empowered Public Service operating in a participative philosophy to ensure quality service for clients—the public."

The State of Minnesota has recently embarked on a "customer focus" initiative that includes both participation and empowerment.

The Province of Saskatchewan in Canada has developed a similar program to increase innovation and client service for the public.

These examples represent the tip of the iceberg. Federal, state, and municipal administration represents a significant percentage of the working population. What the automobile industry faced in the 1980s will happen to these organizations in the 1990s. The answer will be the same. Increased involvement and empowerment will be a chosen strategy to address the issues of workforce reduction, declining budgets, and increased demand for quality of service.

■ ————————— **PREDICTION 2** ————————— ■

Participative Management Will Be Institutionalized by Organizations Currently Embarking on a Shift of Philosophy

Participative management is currently being introduced to organizations as complementary or supplementary to current practices. The future will see the institutionalization of participative management as the current practice. Participative management will change from *a* way of doing things to *the* way of life in the organization. Honda and Toyota have institutionalized participative management so that work is designed to assume participation and involvement. Team meetings are a way of life for workers. In the early phases of participative management, team meetings are scheduled outside of work hours and are seen as alternatives to work. The transition time will be three to five years, depending on the degree of resistance within the system and the degree of leadership provided by the organization.

The Baldridge awards are made by the U.S. government to reward excellence and quality in American firms. Xerox and the Cadillac division of General Motors have been recent winners. In examining the criteria for success, the Baldridge committee clearly examines the degree of institutionalizing that exists for teams, participation, and empowerment. The committee examines the systems that are in place, not simply the enthusiasm exhibited by the organization. This provision of a measurement will be extremely valuable for organizations that will need to learn how to convert participative management from a program to a process.

■   **PREDICTION 3**   ■

Business and Engineering Schools Will Have to Change Their Curriculum to Include Participative Management

Enlightened universities are already changing what and how they teach. The future success of graduates will depend on their ability to work with people as much as on their technical skills. The cultural shock faced by graduates when they begin their careers is unnecessary. We see organizations, such as Shell Canada, investing a large amount of time and money to acclimatize new graduates to the realities of organizational life. Edward de Bono, in his book *Teaching Thinking* (Penguin Press, 1976), makes a powerful argument about the inappropriate focus on learning "things" instead of "thinking." His book focuses on the inability of students to be innovative because of the "right answer" syndrome of the educational system. The same argument can be made about the lack of social skills development and learning how to learn that exists in current educational institutions. Universities' reward system (grades) is focused on individual results. Students learn that it is "me against the exam" and "me against the term paper," and it should be no surprise that difficulties will occur when they enter a participative management workplace. The concepts of sharing, teams, and being rewarded for team results are fundamental changes for those students.

Participative management in the 1990s cannot be simply a course in the curriculum (e.g., Participative Management 101). It will become a way of learning the other technical material necessary for graduation. We foresee business schools that use teams as a basis for learning. Grades will be given to teams, not individuals, for some projects. We see values as being part of what is used to establish learning contracts with students. These changes, for some institutions of higher learning, will impact the professors in the same way current organizational leaders have been impacted by the participative management philosophy.

■ **PREDICTION 4** ■

Participative Management Will Probably Change Its Name to Reflect Another Guru's Interpretation

Participative management has existed under various names since the 1950s. The Tavistock Institute wrote about a concept of social consultancy in the 1950s. The 1960s saw participative management in various leadership programs, such as the Managerial Grid. The 1970s brought us the term "quality of work life." In the 1980s, the term "sociotechnical systems" was coined. Participative management is the cornerstone of all of these and will probably be encapsulated under a new title in the 1990s.

North America idolizes newness and state-of-the-art technologies. Solid concepts are often discarded for theories that are deemed important because of the freshness of the ink. In the 1980s, over 2,500 books were published in the field of business management and leadership. Although participative management will continue, you may have to search for it under a new and marketable title.

CONCLUSION

If you have reached this point in the book, thank you! We hope that some of our insights and experiences will help you in your struggle to understand and apply participative management. As you run up against roadblocks and get discouraged because the obviousness of participative management is being resisted, please remember the following words of advice:

> If the worst thing that happens to you is that the organization expects you to work together and be accountable for what you do, life isn't that bad!

APPENDIXES

Although appendixes do not usually have introductions, we want to explain that our appendixes include the following:

- Tools developed by ourselves and by organizations to address issues we have discussed in this book
- Relevant examples of some of the successes and innovative approaches undertaken by organizations with which we have been involved
- A list of references, primarily books, that we have discussed and that we view as helpful.

As workers and managers attempt to increase participation, they frequently need examples to help their thought process. We caution readers that some of our examples represent what was right for the particular situation being addressed. You cannot copy someone else's vision or values (tempting though that may be) and say, "This is ours." The discovery process for each organization is invaluable. It provides incredible learnings and eurekas that cannot be conveyed by simply reading a document. We feel that seeing what others have developed provides some insight into what you have to do for yourself.

We want to express our gratitude to our clients for permitting us to share the results of their hard work with our readers. What appears on paper in these appendixes as a product of an individual or a team, does not and cannot reflect accurately the agony and the energy that went into the creation of something that appears as simple as a set of values.

Appendix I

PARTICIPATIVE MANAGEMENT ELEMENTS

One frustration organizations experience early in the participative management process is the realization that jargon reigns supreme. Consultants and theorists have developed a vocabulary that creates confusion. (That's why you hire them—to clarify what they mean.) Terms such as values, vision, mission, philosophy statements, and codes of conduct get thrown around without definition or without establishing relationships. Although we have no ownership of these words, we do have a responsibility to clarify for our clients how we see these terms relating to each other. Figure A.1 is a flowchart that attempts to separate the terminology. We also have included some working tools we have developed, borrowed, or modified.

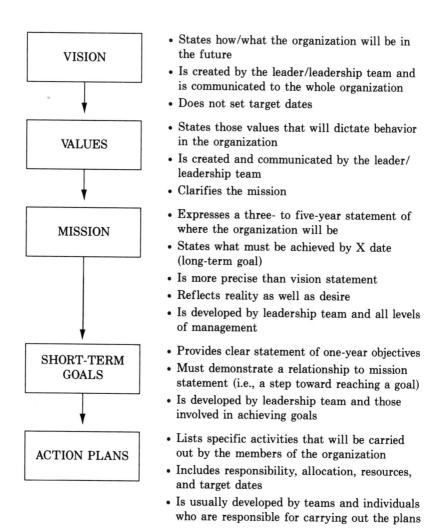

VISION	• States how/what the organization will be in the future • Is created by the leader/leadership team and is communicated to the whole organization • Does not set target dates
VALUES	• States those values that will dictate behavior in the organization • Is created and communicated by the leader/leadership team • Clarifies the mission
MISSION	• Expresses a three- to five-year statement of where the organization will be • States what must be achieved by X date (long-term goal) • Is more precise than vision statement • Reflects reality as well as desire • Is developed by leadership team and all levels of management
SHORT-TERM GOALS	• Provides clear statement of one-year objectives • Must demonstrate a relationship to mission statement (i.e., a step toward reaching a goal) • Is developed by leadership team and those involved in achieving goals
ACTION PLANS	• Lists specific activities that will be carried out by the members of the organization • Includes responsibility, allocation, resources, and target dates • Is usually developed by teams and individuals who are responsible for carrying out the plans

FIGURE A.1 THE TERMINOLOGY OF PARTICIPATIVE MANAGEMENT

VISION

As the cornerstone of the organization's future, a vision is the best attempt of the organization's leaders to express where he or she wants the organization to go. It is *not negotiated* with the organization. Noel Tichy, in his book *Transformational Leadership*, (Wiley, 1989), identifies vision as the leader's responsibility. Other writers go further and suggest it is the leader's *only* job.

Characteristics of a Vision

1. It has to excite people. It should create a fierce desire to want to be part of that vision (i.e., provide a picture in words).

2. It should challenge people—a significant stretch from today.

3. It should describe a state of the "preferred future."

4. It must reflect the beliefs and values of those who create it. The leadership *must* be able to "walk the talk."

5. It must be communicated so that it is pervasive in the organization. People need to be able to relate their plans to the vision.

Examples of Vision Statements

Esso Chemical Canada, Sarnia—Human Resources Division

We will be a customer-focused team of skilled professionals that gains credibility, trust, and respect by utilizing the diversity of our membership, anticipating and sensing the needs of our customers, strategizing our interventions, and ensuring interdependency and consistency within our team. We will be sought out because we deliver what we promise.

General Electric Canada, Inc., Motors and Drive Plant, Peterborough

We will change from a process technology to a people technology by fostering an environment that elicits a high contribution and commitment from employees. Excellence in people will be the new competitive edge. People will provide the superior results the business needs and the leadership to become world class.

Esso Chemicals Canada, Sarnia, Polyethylene Team

We will be a world-class supplier of quality polyethylene as recognized by customers and employees.

Northern Telecom, Inc.

Our company exists to develop and furnish products and systems

- that satisfy our customers' needs and solve their problems
- and that display leadership in quality, value, and technology

to the benefit of our customers and of users, and in the best interests of our employees, our owners, and society.

Correctional Service of Canada

The Correctional Service of Canada, as part of the criminal justice system, contributes to the protection of society by actively encouraging and assisting offenders to become law-abiding citizens, while exercising reasonable, safe, secure, and humane control.

VALUES

Values are currently one of the most popular components in North American organizational life. The rise in popularity is based on two factors:

1. Individuals in society have increased their awareness of their personal values. This creates an upward pressure for the organization to declare what it holds as values.

2. There is an increasing awareness that values represent the basis for all reward and punishment mechanisms. The individual will be rewarded for adherence to certain values and punished for the contravention of other values. Therefore, it is critical that there be a clear statement of values so individuals can modify their behavior appropriately.

Organizational values represent the declared intention of the leadership team. They represent a statement of how the team is willing to be judged internally and externally. The public declaration of values provides the individuals in the organization with two opportunities:

1. To challenge any action by the leader that is in conflict with the stated value. This is extremely courageous of the organization's leaders. Prior to a public disclosure of values, the actions of leaders never had to be defended. It takes guts to say, "Judge my actions according to these values."

2. For individuals to channel their own actions. There should be no further guessing of what will be rewarded or punished. If in all instances customer satisfaction is declared as a value, then every person in contact with the client

must act accordingly. If some individuals cannot accept the values of an organization, they must consider moving to organizations that better reflect their personal values.

There must be consistency between the stated values and the vision statement. If words such as "profitability," "quality," and "empowerment" are found in a vision statement, then it is critical to define values that reflect those visionary ideals. An often repeated phrase in participative management is "walk the talk." The declaration of values represents the "talk that will be walked."

Some of our clients' value statements follow. They are included as examples only and do not represent a judgment of approval or disapproval.

Examples of Values

Correctional Service of Canada
Core Values:

- We respect the dignity of individuals, the rights of all members of society, and the potential for human growth and development.
- We recognize that the offender has the potential to live as a law-abiding citizen.
- We believe that our strength and our major resource in achieving our objectives is our staff and that human relationships are the cornerstone of our endeavor.
- We believe that the sharing of ideas, knowledge, values, and experience, nationally and internationally, is essential to the achievement of our mission.
- We believe in managing the service with openness and integrity and we are accountable to the Solicitor General.

Shell Canada, Scotford Refinery
Basic Values:

- Scotford people are responsible.
- With the necessary information, training and demonstrated skills, individuals can and will make responsible decisions.
- Groups of individuals can work together effectively with minimal supervision.
- People need to grow, advance and contribute to their fullest potential and capability.
- Individuals need recognition.
- It is necessary to have a climate that encourages innovation.
- Errors can provide a constructive learning experience.

Esso Chemical Canada, Sarnia Plant
Values and Guiding Principles:

- Health and safety are paramount.
- We will take the necessary actions to protect the environment and support the community in which we live.
- We will practice open, honest, two-way communications between all levels on all topics.
- People have sufficient information to know, understand, and act on customers' needs.
- We will actively challenge every employee's creativity to continuously improve.
- People who are impacted by decisions will be involved in the making of those decisions.
- We encourage employees to reach their full potential through the design of meaningful work, recognition of contributions, and training and development.

- Leadership is responsive to employee needs, reinforces organizational values, and is consistent in shared focus.

MISSION STATEMENT/LONG-RANGE GOAL

Mission statements are much clearer than vision statements, which represent how the organization wants to be seen in a fairly nonprecise manner (i.e., the preferred future). Mission statements temper idealism with the realities of customers, products, market share, and the other actualities of being in business. Mission statements attempt to tell people where the organization will be in three to five years. As stated earlier, these are also called long-range goals or objectives. The terminology is not important; the applied use is. A mission statement begins the planning process. It creates a need to strategize how to get there.

Characteristics of a Mission Statement

1. It cannot be achieved in one year.
2. It cannot be achieved by one team/person.
3. It includes reference to the key variables used to measure success.
4. It reflects the intent of the vision statement and values.
5. It is usually a short statement, qualified by a list of goal statements.

Examples of Mission Statements

GE Canada Peterborough

- To provide an environment in which our people have the opportunity to realize their full potential through personal and team excellence . . . and to contribute to the success of the business.

- To provide profitable return to meet the expectations of our shareholders.
- To conduct our business in a manner that recognizes our obligations as a good corporate citizen in the community.

Shell Canada, Scotford Refinery

Our mission is to achieve an optimum return on our investment in human and capital resources. Specifically, this mission means that Scotford Refinery's objectives will be to:

- Produce quality products to meet our customers' needs in the marketplace
- Produce these products in the most cost-effective way
- Create a climate that fosters the opportunity for the employee to develop and participate in fulfilling our mission
- Assure that practices recognize our responsibilities for the *protection* of the health and safety of all employees and the environment
- Be a responsible member of the community.

TEAM ACTION PLAN

Table A.1 shows a team action plan made available to us by the HOIS Redesign Team at Esso Chemical Canada's Sarnia Plant. Our thanks to Dave Mathews and the other team members. Although it represents a particular team's plan to achieve job redesign, it is a good example of a long-term plan. We've included this example because it also represents a good model for how to approach job redesign.

TABLE A.1   HOIS REDESIGN TEAM PLAN

PHASE 1   (Timing: February 1990 to June 1990)

Phase 1 concentrated on learning and orientation with respect to team work, work redesign, and the HOIS business. Phase 1 activities included:
- Formation of the redesign team and confirmation of membership
- Team building and development of norms
- Clarification of roles within and outside the redesign team
- Review of boundaries
- Total quality work redesign training
- HOIS organization orientation
- Redesign team goal and measurable outcomes
- Environmental scan and business goals
- Guiding principles
- Quality system orientation
- Planning of site visits and training

PHASE 2   (Timing: June 1990 to October 1990)

Phase 2 concentrated on data collection and included the following activities:
- List the major products and services of the HOIS
- Customer analysis
- Social analysis
- Develop a pareto of opportunities using the business goals, customer, and social analysis data
- Technical analysis on five to six major opportunity areas
- Summarize the data on key variances and opportunities for improvement

PHASE 3   (Timing: October 1990 to January 1991)

Phase 3 concentrated on the development of a macro level redesign plan and included the following activities:
- Macro level redesign plan
- Approval and support from the workers, Joint Industrial Council, performance products management and site steering committee
- Plans to develop the detailed redesign packages in the respective areas

PHASE 4

Phase 4 concentrates on the detailed redesign packages.

PHASE 5

Phase 5 is implementation.

CHARACTERISTICS OF A TEAM LEADER IN PARTICIPATIVE MANAGEMENT

Participative management redefines the role and characteristics of a team leader. Traditionally, leaders were selected with a set of specifications that are totally inappropriate for participative management. Supervisors/leaders who were chosen based on different assumptions have faced great difficulty in changing their behaviors and being successful in participative management. However, many other supervisors have flourished in the changed role. Success or difficulty has to do with the person's style rather than his or her position. In many of our team-building interventions, we have asked teams to list what they consider to be the most significant characteristics of a team leader in a participative management philosophy. What is fascinating to us is the difference between what people feel is necessary and the basis on which supervisors and team leaders actually get selected. The following is a composite of many responses (in no particular rank order):

- Be an effective team player
- Be an effective listener
- Have highly developed interpersonal skills
- Be able to generate trust
- Be able to trust
- Have respect for individuals
- Know the business
- Have excellent coaching skills
- Have excellent confrontational skills
- Be an effective administrator
- Have effective feedback skills

- Have effective meeting skills
- Be an effective defender of the team for the rest of the organization
- Be an effective goal setter and planner
- Be an effective decision maker
- Be an effective trainer
- Be able to challenge ideas/issues instead of people
- Be fair and consistent
- Assume responsibility (with the team) to address deviant team member behavior.

CHARACTERISTICS OF A TEAM MEMBER IN PARTICIPATIVE MANAGEMENT

Often in team-building situations, much time and effort are spent on clarifying the roles of the team's key players. When this is finished, the rest of the team is identified as being in the role of team members. For many individuals, it is not clear as to what this means. They wonder what responsibilities they have and what behaviors are expected. The following is a composite list of characteristics (in no particular rank order) created by various client groups.

- Be open to feedback
- Accept responsibility for the members' behaviors
- Provide feedback to other team members
- Be concerned about winning
- Be willing to personally lose on some issues
- Be willing to confront and stand up on issues
- Be able to confront issues, *not* people

CHARACTERISTICS OF A TEAM MEMBER

- Be a good listener
- Be willing to challenge the status quo
- Be willing to accept learning as a goal
- Be willing to accept responsibility for team members' behavior.

Appendix II

MANAGING
PARTICIPATION MODEL

We have repeated, at the risk of boredom, the belief that the issue of managing effective involvement in decisions is the cornerstone of participative management. In several places in the book, we described the three levels/styles of decision involvement. Figure A.2 is a summary model of the principles in a succinct synopsis. The model is brazenly simple and yet deceptively difficult. The readers who understand this classification of types of involvement have the basis of introducing participative management at the team level. The model attempts to ensure the following:

- Clear definition of those issues that will be dealt with by the leader without fear of challenge by team members (levels 1 and 2)
- Clear definition of those issues that require input before resolution (levels 3 and 4)
- Clear definition of empowerment so teams/individuals are not "second guessed" by managers (levels 5 and 6).

MANAGING PARTICIPATION MODEL

LEVEL E6—EMPOWER A GROUP

Key Factors
1. Group is willing to accept the responsibility.
2. You are willing to relinquish responsibility.
3. Group has skills to make decision.
4. Guidelines are provided.
5. Commitment concern exceeds quality concern.

EXPECT A DECISION

(E) EMPOWERED

DECISION-MAKING STYLE

LEVEL E5—EMPOWER AN INDIVIDUAL

Key Factors
1. Individual is willing to accept responsibility.
2. You are willing to relinquish responsibility.
3. Guidelines are provided.
4. Commitment concern exceeds adequacy concern.
5. Individual has skills to make the decision.

LEVEL C4—MAKE DECISION YOURSELF
BUT ASK FOR HELP

Key Factors
1. You are responsible.
2. Organization accepts that responsibility.
3. You are willing to be influenced.
4. Multiple input/discussion will help.

EXPECT A RECOMMENDATION

(C) COLLABORATIVE

DECISION-MAKING STYLE

LEVEL C3—MAKE DECISION YOURSELF
BUT ASK INDIVIDUALS FOR HELP

Key Factors
1. You are responsible.
2. Organization accepts that responsibility.
3. You are willing to be influenced.
4. Individuals can help.

LEVEL I2—MAKE DECISION YOURSELF
BUT CHECK THE FACTS FIRST

Key Factors
1. You are responsible.
2. Organization accepts that responsibility.
3. You lack facts to make the decision.

EXPECT INFORMATION

(I) INDEPENDENT

DECISION-MAKING STYLE

LEVEL I1—MAKE DECISION YOURSELF

Key Factors
1. You are responsible to make decision.
2. Organization accepts that responsibility.
3. You possess all data.

EXPECT COMPLIANCE

INCREASING PARTICIPANT COMMITMENT

FIGURE A.2   A PARTICIPATIVE LEADERSHIP MODEL

Appendix III

TEAM EFFECTIVENESS

Throughout this book, we have referred to a team effectiveness model. The following guide is the translation of that model into a structured sequence for team discussion. It is particularly useful in the formation stages of team development. Teams that are effectively operating on an ongoing basis can refer to the guide to assess their performance, but would not necessarily refer to it daily.

Task

- What is our long-term goal?
- Are we all committed to that goal?
- What is our short-term goal?
- Do we agree?
- What are we going to achieve today?
- Is our mandate to decide or recommend?

Roles

- What structural roles do we need to create (e.g., scribe, timekeeper, chairperson, facilitator)?
- Why are we each here? What is expected of me, and what do I expect of other members (e.g., information source, expert role, alternate generator, decision maker)?

Process

- What is our agenda?
- How should we structure our discussions?

- How will we handle decisions (e.g., consensus, majority vote, unanimity, referred to higher level)?

Relationships

- Do we have past history of conflict that we need to address?
- Are people representing themselves or functions?
- Are values in conflict?
- Are norms necessary to ensure effectiveness?

Appendix IV

GROUP PROCESS
OBSERVATION GUIDE

An effective team must be aware of how it is performing. A heart transplant team in a hospital does not await the patient's recovery or demise to assess effectiveness. Similarly, business teams need to keep track of how they are progressing, as well as measure the output. The Group Process Observation tool was developed to permit the specific monitoring of a group in action. It can be used by any member of the team or an objective outsider to identify the team's strengths and weaknesses. As with other tools in the Appendixes, feel free to use, adapt, or ignore this one.

GROUP PROCESS OBSERVATION

A. **TASK CLARIFICATION**	Group determines the goal/task facing them in this particular situation.
Questions	**Observations**
1. Was the goal/task clearly presented?	
2. Was it imposed or discussed?	
3. Was the task/goal accepted?	
4. Was the task/goal referred to during discussions to assist progress?	
5. Was it used to test group results?	
B. **ROLE CLARIFICATION**	Members identify their contributions and establish roles they will play. Why are they there?
Questions	**Observations**
1. Did participants discuss their respective roles?	
2. Was there acceptance of those roles?	
3. Was there role consistency throughout the discussion?	
4. What kinds of roles were identified?	
C. **LEADERSHIP CLARIFICATION**	Group identifies the nature of leadership required to achieve the goal.
Questions	**Observations**
1. Was the appropriateness of a leadership style discussed?	
2. Was the leadership shared?	
3. Did the group accept the responsibility to help the leader?	
4. What leadership style was used?	

D. PROBLEM SOLVING AND DECISION MAKING	Members agree on the best method of approaching the situation facing the group. How should we go about it?

Questions	Observations
1. Was there a full discussion of the facts prior to solutions?	
2. Were facts verified or challenged?	
3. Was there a discussion on how to approach the situation?	
4. What means of reaching agreement was used? • Consensus • Majority • Unanimity • Imposition	
5. Is there commitment to the solution?	

E. CONFLICT RESOLUTION	Group discusses how to resolve conflict should it arise.

Questions	Observations
1. Did conflict occur?	
2. What was the basis of conflict?	
3. What tactics were used to address this conflict?	
4. Did the group accept responsibility or leave it to the leader?	
5. How effectively was it handled?	

F. FEEDBACK AND ANALYSIS	Members determine how success will be measured in terms of progress toward the goal.

Questions	Observations
1. Did group stop and assess progress periodically?	
2. Was there a focus on both positive and negative points?	

Questions	Observations
3. Was the group open to critique?	
4. Did any change in behavior/procedure occur?	

G. **NORM DEVELOPMENT**	Group identifies any necessary behavioral guidelines.

Questions	Observations
1. Did the group/leader discuss behavioral guidelines?	
2. Was there discussion?	
3. Was there acceptance?	
4. Were norms used to facilitate progress?	
5. What norms were seen in action?	

Note: Norms can rarely be assessed from one meeting. They can be observed by the actions of the participants.

H. **OVERALL CLIMATE**	Group observes contributing or hindering factors that influenced group success.

Questions	Observations
1. Was there freedom of participation and expression?	
2. Did there seem to be a sense of shared concern?	
3. Were feelings explored as well as facts?	
4. Was there any sense of challenge and fun?	

Types of Groups and Teams

Table A.2 explores different ways that work and people are organized. A full description of each is found on Chapter 4.

TABLE A.2 TYPES OF TEAMS

	1 Natural Work Groups	2 Natural Work Teams	3 Integrated Teams	4 Short-Term Task Forces	5 Long-Term Task Forces and Committees
Membership	Specialists	Specialists + work groups	All individuals necessary to do job	Appointed or voluntary Fixed time frame	Appointed/voluntary Long-term fixed time frame
Leadership	Based on expertise or organizational level	Formal leader/manager role is exercised	Formal leader/coordinator role is exercised Can rotate—dependent on task/situation	Usually leader controlled	Usually based on position or level in organization Usually a formal "chair"
Relationships	Independent action by individuals	Independent individuals relate more to leader	Totally interactive between individuals	All have full-time jobs outside of task force Collegial but only in task	Infrequent but usually intense
Rewards	Based on individual performance	Mainly individual Some group rewards	Team-based rewards Pay for knowledge and skill	Usually team based	Usually not considered
Process	Goals and process controlled by leader	Goals/process controlled by leader	Team sets own goals and negotiates with management	Usually imposed but could be negotiated	Designed into committee structure/goals

Appendix VI

MEETINGS

Participative management inevitably means meetings. Whether an organization's thrust is toward increased involvement or fully integrated teams, there is a need for meetings to happen and be successful. This appendix provides some tools we have found to be successful in improving the meeting skills of team leaders and members. We extend particular thanks to Trevor Jordan of Polysar Rubber for his help in developing these tools. This appendix includes the following tools:

- Characteristics of a Good Agenda
- Agenda Planning Worksheet
- Meeting Process Planner

CHARACTERISTICS OF A GOOD AGENDA

1. Distributed to all participants
2. Distributed sufficiently prior to meeting to allow preparation
3. Includes:

   a. Overall purpose

   b. Start time

   c. Completion time

   d. Location

   e. List of participants/roles (if appropriate)

   f. Sequence of items

   g. Timing allocated for specific items

   h. Objectives/output expected for each item

   i. Information required for each agenda item
4. Provides for a summary of action plans and requirements
5. *It is followed and managed for success*

AGENDA PLANNING WORKSHEET

Purpose

Specific results required to achieve meeting purpose:

1.
2.

Type of Meeting

Problem Solving _____ Creative Problem Solving _____

Situational Review _____ Planning _____

Decision Making _____ Information Sharing _____

Combination _____

When

Where

Who

Participants and roles if appropriate (e.g., information source, decision maker, facilitator):

AGENDA FOR THE ACTUAL MEETING

(Sequence of activities to achieve objectives)

1. Introduction
   - Personal introductions/roles
   - Review—purpose/objectives/importance
   - Situational expectations

   Agenda Items (activity, time, responsibility)

2.

3.

4.

5. Summary of Decisions/Actions (what, who, when in relation to objective)

MEETING PROCESS PLANNER

Stage 1. *Preparation*

1. Is the meeting necessary?
2. What goals/results do we hope to achieve?
3. Is a meeting the best way to achieve them?
4. What agenda is required?
5. Who needs to attend?
6. What roles will each play?
7. How will I communicate goals/roles to them?
8. What is the best time to hold the meeting?
9. How much time do I need for the meeting?
10. What physical facilities/arrangements are needed?
11. What information will be needed?
12. How can I ensure that the information will be available?

Stage 2. *Approach*

Situation:

1. Which type of meeting is required in order to meet the goal?
2. Is input/acceptance by others necessary?
3. Is the required data available?
4. Is there severe time pressure?

Participants:

5. What is their level of relevant knowledge/experience?
6. What is their level of interest?

7. What is their level of maturity as a group?

8. Do they prefer to function in a dependent or independent mode?

9. What role do they expect me to play?

10. What role do they expect to play?

11. Are there existing conflicts among them or with me?

12. Are there vested interests?

Myself:

13. With what approach am I most comfortable?

14. What is my role: advocate, pleader, facilitator, final decider?

15. What leadership style is most appropriate?

16. Am I the best choice to lead the meeting?

17. Is an independent process facilitator required?

Stage 3. Conduct

1. Pinpoint the purpose.

2. Clarify goals/results expected.

3. Review/adjust agenda and timings.

4. Facilitate/control participation/member input.

5. Keep discussion on track and summarize progress.

6. Manage the time.

7. Manage member roles/critical actors.

8. Test for and confirm agreement and decisions.

9. Confirm action steps and responsibilities.

10. Record decision and planned action and responsibility.

Stage 4. Supportive Behavior

1. Be aware of and accept the feelings of yourself and others.
2. Encourage others to express ideas and opinions.
3. Pay attention to group and individual needs/goals.
4. Pay attention to both process and content.
5. Respect and explore areas of disagreement.
6. Encourage members to explore. inquire, initiate, and be innovative.
7. Be willing to seek and provide data and opinions.
8. Be willing to compromise.
9. Help to define and clarify issues.
10. Help to develop and test standards.
11. Be willing to give and receive feedback.
12. Develop and inspire an atmosphere of trust.
13. Maintain harmony within disagreement.
14. Be willing to praise.
15. Avoid attacking and defending.

Appendix VII

TYPES OF PROCESSES TO RESOLVE TEAM SITUATIONS

In Chapter 5, we discussed how teams work. In one section, we described the need for teams to agree on the process/procedure that they would use to achieve their goal. This appendix provides some sample processes that are used by effective teams. These are modifications from *The Proactive Manager* by Lorne Plunkett and Guy Hale (Wiley, 1981). We have adapted these ideas to reflect the concept of participative management and the need for teams to have a planned sequence of steps in a meeting. The underlying principle is that different team discussions will have to follow different agendas.

The following processes are described:

- Problem solving—Isolating a cause of a problem that has occurred.
- Decision making—Choosing a course of action.
- Planning/implementation—Ensuring that decisions are successful when put into action.
- Creative problem solving—Generating new and different solutions to existing problems.
- Situation review—Sorting out a range of issues and identifying action plans to resolve them.

Teams need some form of structure to be successful. Discussion without direction should be restricted to group therapy. For each process, the following items are provided:

- An agenda for discussing the issue
- The "getting started" questions to ensure effective involvement and readiness
- A flowchart of the process to be used.

AGENDA FOR PROBLEM SOLVING MEETING

1. Get agreement on the title or statement of the problem and goal of the meeting.

2. Describe the problem.

3. Use the problem description to probe for clues.

4. List changes and possible causes.

5. Test for causes.

6. Develop verification plan.

7. Arrange for feedback.

GETTING STARTED: PROBLEM SOLVING

1. What is the problem to be solved?

2. How did the problem become identified?

3. What checking has been done to verify the existence of the problem?

4. What, if any, action has already been taken to address the problem?

5. When is an answer required?

6. What do you want the solution to achieve?

GETTING STARTED: PROBLEM SOLVING

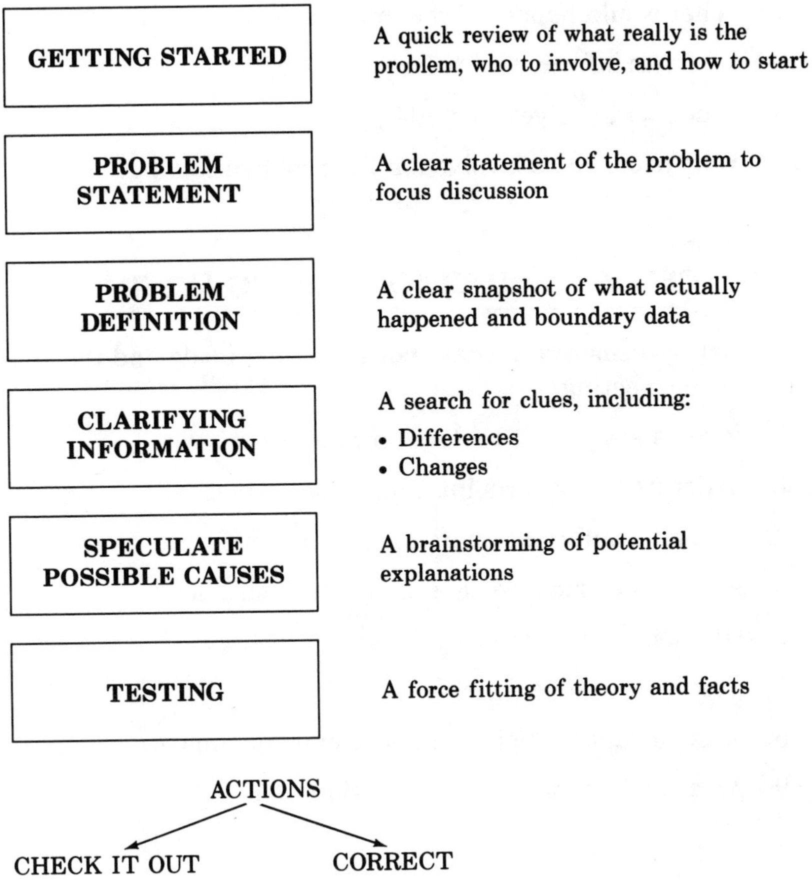
GETTING STARTED
A quick review of what really is the problem, who to involve, and how to start
PROBLEM STATEMENT
A clear statement of the problem to focus discussion
PROBLEM DEFINITION
A clear snapshot of what actually happened and boundary data
CLARIFYING INFORMATION
A search for clues, including:
• Differences
• Changes
SPECULATE POSSIBLE CAUSES
A brainstorming of potential explanations
TESTING
A force fitting of theory and facts
ACTIONS
CHECK IT OUT
CORRECT

FIGURE A.3 PROBLEM SOLVING FLOWCHART

7. What would happen if the problem is not solved?

8. Who has information to help resolve it?

9. When will you get started?

10. Who needs to be involved in the problem solving?

AGENDA FOR DECISION-MAKING MEETING

1. Get agreement on what choice is being made and the goal of the meeting.

2. Involve key people to develop relevant criteria.

3. Separate the criteria into limits/desirables.

4. Assemble information on the performance of options.

5. Assess performance against limits/desirables.

6. Develop and list relevant risks.

7. Assess and judge the risks.

8. Make balanced choice and develop communication plan.

9. Arrange for monitoring and action plan.

GETTING STARTED: DECISION MAKING

1. What choice are you trying to make?

2. Is it your responsibility to recommend _____?

   decide _____?

3. What created the need for this decision?

GETTING STARTED	A quick review of what is being decided and who should be involved
DECISION STATEMENT	A clear direction to provide focus and generate options
DECISION FACTORS	A list of requirements for this decision
DECISION OPTIONS	A list and assessment of the courses of action that are open
RISK ANALYSIS	A list and assessment of those risks that could occur for any considered option
CHOICE	A balancing of risk and performance

FIGURE A.4   DECISION MAKING FLOWCHART

4. What other decisions were considered/made?

5. What would happen if "no decision" was made?

6. Who will ultimately have to approve this decision?

7. By when must the decision be made?

8. Who needs to be involved in making the decision?

9. Who will need to be consulted prior to making the decision?

10. How will you communicate the progress and the decision to the involved parties?

AGENDA FOR PLANNING IMPLEMENTATION MEETING

1. Get agreement on the goal/objective of the task and of this meeting.

2. List key events/activities required to achieve the goal.

3. Assign responsibility, sequence and target dates for each event/activity.

4. List key potential problems and assess for risks.

5. List key likely causes and assess for probability.

6. Develop preventive actions for key likely causes.

7. Develop a backup plan with triggers for major potential problems.

8. Chart plan and communicate.

9. Develop monitoring and plan management responsibility and mileposts.

GETTING STARTED: PLANNING IMPLEMENTATION

1. What exactly are you going to implement?

2. Have all appropriate decisions been made to permit progress?

3. Who will be affected by this plan and implementation?

4. How will you gain their support and involvement?

5. Who needs to be involved as part of the implementation team?

GETTING STARTED	A quick review of what is to be implemented, who should be involved, and how to start
PLAN DEVELOPMENT	A listing of the necessary activities to achieve the goal, with responsibility and target dates assigned
PLAN ASSESSMENT	A review of the key potential problems and their likely causes
PLAN PROTECTION	The development of preventive and contingent actions
MANAGE THE PLAN	The establishment of mileposts and review points

FIGURE A.5   PLANNING/IMPLEMENTATION FLOWCHART

6. How will you arrange for feedback and communication to involved parties?

7. By when must it be implemented?

AGENDA FOR CREATIVE PROBLEM-SOLVING MEETING

1. Get agreement on the goals of the meeting.

2. List and test the proposed opportunity statement.

3. Develop a list of end result opportunity requirements.

4. Use brain teaser/mind loosening exercise (if required).

5. Generate ideas with group.

6. Perform preliminary assessment and combination of ideas.

7. Combine and develop solution.

8. Test feasibility/performance of solution.

9. Develop action plan for verification and implementation.

10. Develop monitoring and feedback plan.

GETTING STARTED: CREATIVE PROBLEM SOLVING

1. What opportunity is being addressed?

2. What are three other ways to state the opportunity?

    •

    •

    •

3. Which of the above statements of opportunity best describes the starting point?

4. Who will be affected by this opportunity, and how will we include their concerns?

5. Who should be involved in the generation of solutions?

6. Are we:

    • Recommending solutions?____

    • Empowered to implement solutions?____

7. Is some form of "loosening up" required prior to idea generation?

8. Which idea generation techniques should we use?

DEVELOP INNOVATION STATEMENT	The clarification statement of the opportunity to be addressed
DEVELOP DESIGN CRITERIA	Listing of the key constraints and results required
SELECT KEY DESIGN CRITERIA	Choosing those criteria that will yield possible solutions
GENERATE IDEAS	The freewheeling development on unjudged solutions
SELECT AND COMBINE IDEAS	A preliminary review and assessment of ideas
EVALUATE IDEAS	An analytical review for feasibility and performance
MODIFY AND DEVELOP SOLUTION	Evaluation of surviving ideas into a cohesive solution
PLAN AND IMPLEMENT SOLUTION	Planning and protecting the solution

FIGURE A.6   CREATIVE PROBLEM SOLVING FLOWCHART

AGENDA FOR SITUATION REVIEW MEETING

1. Get agreement on goals of the meeting.

2. Develop list of issues and concerns that this group has to address.

3. Break large problems into manageable concerns.

4. Assess priority of problems.

5. Develop action plan for resolution of key problems. Include responsibility, timing, and starting point of resolution.

GETTING STARTED	The consideration of who to involve and what to consider
LIST AND ASSESS CONCERNS	The identification of action items and determination of their status
CONCERNS REFINEMENT (OPTIONAL)	Breaking concerns down to actionable size
PRIORITIZE	Determination of the order of handling concerns to maximize time usage
ASSIGN ACTION AND RESPONSIBILITY	Determination of the first step and assigning responsibility to getting started

FIGURE A.7 SITUATION REVIEW FLOWCHART

Appendix VIII

A CASE STUDY ON
SOME OF THE ISSUES

We thought we would end this book with a case study to bring together many of the concepts we have discussed. Although the Pan-American Rubber Company is fictionalized, some events that are described represent real issues we have encountered in a wide range of clients.

Following the case study, we pose questions you need to answer. We have provided a sample analysis that identifies some typical solutions to the issues that exist in Pan-American. Your answers might be better! The key is not the need to be right, as much as the need to resolve some of the issues if participative management, customer service, and quality management are to be successful.

PAN-AMERICAN RUBBER COMPANY CASE STUDY

Pan-American Rubber Company is a major supplier of rubber and other petrochemical products to Canadian and American manufacturers. The company is located in Clearwater, Michigan, in the heart of a major petrochemical and manufacturing complex. Over the years, Pan-Am has enjoyed a preeminent reputation in the rubber industry for quality products and quality customer relations.

Three years ago, Pan-Am introduced a total quality program in its manufacturing operation. This program has been accompanied by a new focus on participative management, which means that people at lower levels in the organization are asked to assume more responsibility for the production and shipment of products and for customer satisfaction. This emphasis has resulted in a strengthening of customer relationships and has significantly enhanced the company's market share.

The marketing manager of Pan-Am (see Figure A.3 for the plant's organizational chart) faces a problem that needs immediate resolution with Freestone Tire, a key customer of one of Pan-Am's major products for many years. The relationship has been very strong and as positive as the relationship with any other tire manufacturer. Pan-Am has cooperated fully with Freestone in developing unique formulations to meet their product specifications and has cooperated in a "just-in-time" inventory supply system.

Yesterday, the marketing manager was informed that a major problem has developed in the relationship between Pan-Am and Freestone. The weekly shipment of twenty-six skids of rubber to Freestone's Joliet manufacturing plant had left the plant on time. However, samples taken by Freestone lab technicians upon arrival indicated that two of the twenty-six skids were "off spec" and, as a result, Freestone refused to accept all twenty-six skids. A standard operating procedure for handling customer complaints and client shipment rejections was then put into effect. Immediately, a new production run of a further twenty-six skids was shipped to Joliet to ensure no loss of production at Freestone.

The Pan-Am account representative for Freestone, upon hearing about the problem, immediately asked for and was given the sample results taken before shipment. All indications were that the shipment was "on spec" before being shipped to Freestone. A field technical representative was sent to Joliet to obtain samples from the two skids in question. These samples were sent to the lab at Freestone: One sample was marginally off spec (but could have been used), and the other sample was found to be fully within specification.

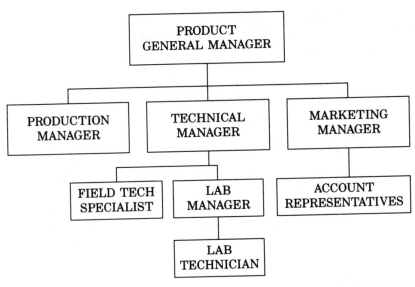

FIGURE A.8   ORGANIZATIONAL CHART OF PAN-AM RUBBER COMPANY

When the Pan-Am lab results were communicated to the lab technician at Freestone, "all hell broke loose." The customer accused Pan-Am of doctoring the sample, and the account representative was upset over the apparently confrontational approach taken by Pan-Am lab people. The Pan-Am field technical representative blamed Freestone for using poor lab procedures and stated that Pan-Am lab technicians had retested the samples and confirmed their original findings.

The marketing manager asked both representative parties to submit their understanding of the situation and scheduled a meeting with all the relevant parties to determine an effective response and to resolve the problem.

The marketing manager's objective is to increase market share and to improve the profit contribution of this product. Freestone is a key customer in attaining these goals. Pan-Am is facing a particularly delicate situation because a competitor has been aggressively marketing its quality leadership in the field of rubber production.

The marketing manager believes strongly that the firm's marketing goals have been significantly enhanced because of product quality and the customer focus that has developed over the last two years by marketing, production, and technical staff. The increased communication between labs, production, sales, and the customer has removed the bottlenecks that used to occur because account managers were the only ones who talked to customers.

Based on the above background and the following memos, if you were the marketing manager, what would you do in relation to these questions?

1. What issues are you facing?

2. What would be the purpose of the meeting that you are planning?

3. Whom would you invite and why?

4. Who will be responsible for any decisions that might be made?

MEMO

TO: Marketing Manager

FROM: The Freestone Account Representative (for Pan-
Am Rubber)

In summarizing my knowledge and awareness of the situation, I would like to communicate the following to you:

1. As part of my ongoing representation with Freestone, I have regularly visited the client and have developed an excellent working relationship with their purchasing manager. He and I share common interests, and I usually have the opportunity to meet with him socially as well as professionally. Jack and I usually try to get in at least two rounds of golf a year when I visit Joliet.

2. It has been my goal to increase the sales volume, particularly with Freestone. As you remember at our last pricing meeting, I thought we would have to reduce prices to maintain our volume and business with Freestone. However, the consensus was that price reductions were out of the question and, therefore, the best we could do for Freestone was to maintain last year's prices.

3. There has been a significant push on attaining quality leadership with our products. If price cannot become the basis for maintaining client relationships, then obviously quality and customer focus has got to

be our major concern. I am fully aware of, and have participated in, some of the quality programs that have been introduced within the production facility. Although I understand the concepts, I find them a bit difficult to accept. I am confused by all this quality mumbo jumbo.

4. The total customer supplier team approach that we have adopted has led to an increased level of contact between the technical staff and our customers. I must point out that this has created some difficulty for me as the account representative. Life was much simpler when I was the only contact between the client and the customer. If I had been the contact person and had been able to talk to my friend Jack at Freestone, I doubt very much that this blowup would have occurred. I am concerned with how things are presented to the customer. Perhaps with the focus on participative management and statistical process control, some work should be done on interpersonal skills if lab technicians are asked to talk to customers.

MEMO

TO: Marketing Manager

FROM: Technical Manager

   I have worked with Pan-Am Rubber for some time and have been responsible for both the process lab and the quality control aspects of manufacturing. I have been excited about the new emphasis on quality and have been eager to pursue and put some of these new principles to work, particularly the concept of getting closer to the customer. As a result of this focus, I have worked closely with the lab technicians in Joliet and have noticed that there has been a shift in results between the labs in the last year. Working with the field technical specialist, I have discovered that the introduction of a modified carbon black, which is used in compounding samples, has been introduced into our lab in the last year. The result of this has been a much more consistent sampling result, which has improved the quality that we ship from the plant. Details such as this have not been communicated to either the account manager or you, but I don't see this as being the level of detail with which you need to be involved.

   I personally take great pride in the quality of the lab and the testing process. In a competitive situation such as with Freestone, it is critical to be able to prove quality as well as to ship quality. Last year seemed to be one of continual improvement in client relations. In fact, it has been critical for us to maintain ongoing relationships with the client's lab people, particularly because of high turnover in lab staff at Freestone. Last week, when you called about

this particular shipment, there was another new lab technician on the line, and it was quite obvious that no amount of
discussion would cause him to listen. Our having to break-
in and retrain Freestone staff seems to be an ongoing situation, and it looks as though we will have to start over
again. I know that you take great pride in your staff and
the results they have achieved, but I hope that the meeting
you have called does not deteriorate into finger pointing at
my staff and their test procedures.

MEMO

TO: Marketing Manager

FROM: Field Technical Specialist

In response to your request, I am including my understanding and information about the Freestone situation.

As a field technical specialist, my job is to work closely with the customer at their site. Freestone has been a major account for me, and I have worked closely with their plant people, the lab technicians, and the chief chemist. The chief chemist is a personal friend, and he and I agree on most issues that need to be resolved. As a matter of fact, in several instances, I have been very helpful to Freestone with suggestions for improving their production quality. Six months ago, I helped them by modifying their recipe for the rubber to counteract a low cure rate that had come to the attention of Freestone staff. Suggestions such as these have been greatly appreciated by the client because they are better able to meet their production quotas under tight time constraints.

I believe there is a bias in the Freestone sampling process. Freestone tests consistently show a higher result (results indicating that the product deviates from an acceptable standard) than our tests. Although the bias has been high, it has usually been within specifications.

I hope this information is of help to you. I am anxious to get involved in resolving this situation.

MEMO

TO: Marketing Manager

FROM: Lab Tech 1

As requested, I am submitting the information that I have on the Freestone situation.

It was my job to complete the original testing on the Freestone product before it was shipped. In the lab tests that I conducted, the results showed that the product was within specification prior to shipping to Joliet.

I completed my training as a lab technician four weeks ago. I am very concerned about the accuracy of lab results, and consequently followed procedures exactly as I was trained and even checked my results with my senior lab technician to make sure that they were correct.

I have no further information for you other than I know the product was on spec when it was shipped.

MEMO

TO: Marketing Manager

FROM: Lab Tech 2

As requested, I am submitting the information that you requested about the Freestone shipment.

I have worked in this lab for over 20 years and by now I could do most of the tests with my eyes closed. I am also responsible for monitoring and assisting new technicians. I must compliment the training process because the quality of people coming into the labs is extremely high. In fact, lab tech 1 is very, very good and has no problems with seeking advice and support when he has questions.

It was my responsibility to test the sample that was returned from Freestone, and I have no doubt that it was within specification. One shipment was a little high in the spec range, but within the normal limits. This is not the first time that I have been involved in a Freestone problem, and I am sure that if I could go down to Joliet and work with their lab technicians, I could clean up the problem very quickly. Too often these problems are approached at the management and sales levels, when lab technicians working with lab technicians would solve the problem.

I would suggest that I go to Joliet. In two days we could resolve this problem. I know that with the current staff shortage in the lab and the increased volume of testing, the workload would make it difficult for me to get away, but if we truly believe in quality, and participation, I think we have got to look at the workload and the involvement of lab techs in solving customer problems.

SAMPLE ANALYSIS SHEET FOR
PAN-AMERICAN RUBBER CASE STUDY

■   QUESTION 1   ■

What Issues Are You Facing?

As in any situation, more than one issue faces the marketing manager. Some of these situations are interconnected and will be ignored unless they are separated into specific concerns. The process of situation review (see Appendix VII) should be used to isolate the different concerns.

Sample List of Concerns

Issue 1. Freestone has returned twenty-six skids of rubber because samples failed at Freestone Labs.

   a. Replacement shipment has been sent as per standard customer service procedures, and no action is necessary to ensure that Freestone has an adequate supply of raw material.

   b. There is a discrepancy between sample test results at Pan-American and Freestone labs.

   Action Needed: Determine cause of discrepancy.

   c. Client relations have been damaged because of the finger pointing by both parties when the two companies' lab technicians communicated.

   Action Needed: Determine the cause of the communication problem and develop some form of corrective action.

   d. We need to determine how best to reestablish our relationship with the client for long-term business.

Action Needed: Develop short-term and long-term response to Freestone.

Issue 2. There seem to be very different perceptions of what is meant by participative management within Pan-Am. This is creating communication problems within the company and with clients.

a. The account manager doesn't appear to have understood or accepted some basic principles of participative management. He calls it "mumbo jumbo" and also wants his world of client contacts not to be affected by a move to participative management.

   Action Needed: If participative management is to be successful, the account manager will have to accept the changed responsibility of production and lab people.

b. The technical manager seems to have defined his role in the changed customer focus as the "Lone Ranger." His responsibility for supporting and communicating to his team members at Pan-Am is being ignored. Critical information is being withheld. Participative management requires effective sharing of information downward, upward, and horizontally to peers.

   Action Needed: Clarify the responsibility of the technical manager in relation to sharing information.

c. The field technical specialist seems to confuse client service with "covering up" bad shipments. Short-term service involves helping the client meet the production schedule. Long-term client service involves communicating with one's peers about ongoing problems and avoiding bad shipments.

   Action Needed: Clarify the responsibility of field people in relation to Pan-Am production and lab people.

■ **QUESTION 2** ■

What Would Be the Purpose of the Meeting That You Are Planning?

Since a meeting has been called, it would be appropriate to have a reason. There are several possible purposes:

1. To resolve the Freestone problem
2. To resolve the testing inconsistency problem
3. To resolve the Pan-Am internal problems
4. To develop a Pan-Am approach to resolve the Freestone problem.

1. To resolve the Freestone problem. This is inappropriate as the purpose for the first meeting. Because all the data suggest that Pan-Am needs to get its act together, it would be precipitous to address this purpose. This purpose cannot be achieved without involving representation of Freestone, and it is too early for that involvement. This might be the purpose at the second meeting.

2. To resolve the testing inconsistency problem. This is inappropriate for the same reasons as the first purpose. Freestone would have to be involved, and Pan-Am is not ready for that. It also assumes that the cause of the problem is testing inconsistency. This assumption may be correct, but there are several implications if it is not correct.

3. To resolve the Pan-Am internal problems. This definitely must be done, but not at this meeting. Clarifying the understanding of participative management should never take precedence over meeting customer requirements.

4. To develop a Pan-Am approach to the Freestone problem. This is the starting point. Many decisions need to be made about the best way to reestablish the customer's respect and business. Such issues need to be determined as:

- Do we go there?
- Do they come here?
- Who goes?
- Who should participate?
- What do we know as a starting point to problem solving?
- What additional information needs to be collected?
- Is there additional interim action required to ensure that the problem doesn't escalate?

Who Would You Invite and Why?

The purpose of a meeting dictates the participants. Therefore, there should be no attendees from Freestone at this first meeting, which is about getting Pan-Am's act together. Possible participants from Pan-Am include the following (with the roles they play):

- Marketing manager (chairperson and decision maker)—He or she is the only objective party and has a stake in the outcome. Ultimate decision making, however, is the responsibility of the marketing manager. It is a C4 Decision (see p. 223).
- Account manager (information source and information analyst)—The account manager has a stake in the results. Although he or she knows very little about the specific problem, he or she does know about possible Freestone reactions and should be part of the information analysis function.

- Field technical specialist (information source and information analyst)—He or she is the only one who has seen the product at the Freestone plant. Because of this specialist's close contact, he or she knows more about the testing process and possible Freestone reactions.

- Technical manager (information source and information analyst)—All lab testing and field support is the responsibility of the technical manager. Any change in procedures will require his or her support and analysis.

- Lab technicians 1 and 2 (information sources)—Lab technician 1 has very little information to offer. However, if participative management is part of the way of conducting business, this meeting can be part of his learning experience. It is critical that this technician is not, however, part of the decision-making process. He does not have the required skill or analysis experience.

  Lab technician 2 has very specific information to provide and should have input to the decision-making process. His or her letter seems to indicate a bias toward solving the problem in a very restricted manner—"I will go to Joliet." If no further objectivity is expected, then this person should not have a role as information analyst.

■   **QUESTION 4**   ■

Who Will Be Responsible for Any Decisions That Might Be Made?

The marketing manager will be responsible for the decision. Because he or she needs input and information, it is impossible to make a decision without assistance. However, the data seem to indicate that this group is not yet able to make the necessary decisions, and therefore it cannot go to a group decision.

SELECTED READINGS

We have found the following list of books to be most helpful in our work with clients in recent years. Some are classics, and others represent the most up-to-date thinking by people we consider to be expert in the field. For each book, we provide a brief overview of what the reader should expect to find between the covers. The list is not all-encompassing, but it does form, in our opinions, a solid core of knowledge. We have listed the books in alphabetical order by author.

> Beckhard, Richard, and Harris, Reuban T. *Organizational Transitions, Managing Complex Change,* 2nd ed., (Reading, MA: Addison Wesley, 1977).

The first edition of this book, in 1977, dealt with the change process as it applied to the complexities that affected organizations at that time. In 1977, organizations were largely technology driven, and change occurred within that framework. The second edition has been revised to fit organizations that are now market driven and that are affected by dramatic shifts in orientation. These changes and others have increased significantly the need to create change while maintaining stability with organizations.

Beckhard and Harris offer techniques and advice that are invaluable to anyone considering any form of change. They provide case studies that exemplify how their processes and techniques have been utilized in organizations to carry out needed change strategies. We, and many other practitioners, have adopted (and adapted) these proven techniques to help clients work through the various phases of change. Understanding the change process and how it can be implemented effectively in today's organizations is, in our view, what this book is about.

Block, Peter. *The Empowered Manager*, (San Francisco: Jossey-Bass, 1987).

In this book, Peter Block describes how middle managers can escape the bureaucratic ruts in which they often find themselves and the responsibility for the operation of their businesses. He shows how managers and employees can become empowered and more entrepreneurial in creating the kind of organization in which they would like to work.

Dyer, William G. *Team Building, Issues and Alternatives,* 2nd ed., (Reading, MA: Addison Wesley, 1987).

This is a revised version of Bill Dyer's original book on the subject, written in the 1970s. In this second edition, Dyer writes about the concept of teams and describes in detail the process of team building. He also writes about the different types of teams and offers some excellent advice and techniques for helping teams as they struggle with team issues and their own development. The name Bill Dyer is synonymous with team building.

Harvey, Jerry B. *The Abilene Paradox (and Other Meditations on Management),* (Lexington, MA: Lexington Books, 1988).

Jerry Harvey provides incredible insights to organizational dilemmas. His style of writing is different in that he uses humor (which we could all use more of) to communicate profound concepts that he has developed over his many years of working with organizations. In this book, he describes the inability of organizations to manage agreement, such as a trip to Abilene (when you really wanted to stay home!). He masterfully depicts organizations such as Phrog Farms and uses Japanese airline pilots Adolph Eichmann and Matt Dillon to define problems that rob organizations of their potential for effectiveness. If you like to laugh and learn, this book is worth reading.

Kanter, Rosabeth Moss. *The Change Masters,* (New York: Simon and Schuster, 1983).

Although this book is about energizing innovation and entrepreneurship in America, Chapter 9, "Dilemmas of Participation," is a must read for anyone who is considering teams and participation. Although we found the rest of the book interesting, this chapter alone makes it worthwhile. Kanter's description of dilemmas opened our eyes to the existence and impact of myths.

Kanter supports her ideas with a comprehensive research component. We found it comforting that so many of our conclusions are consistent with her results. The key similarity that bears mention is that the benefits of participation are worth the hassle of confronting myths and dilemmas.

Kouzes, James M., and Posner, Barry Z. *The Leadership Challenge,* (San Francisco: Jossey-Bass, 1987).

In this excellent book, Kouzes and Posner describe the five basic practices and 10 behaviors that are found in exemplary leaders. Their research is developed around leaders they found in today's world, not in history. The book provides a wealth of knowledge about how any manager can lead others to extraordinary contributions.

Lawler, Edward., III. *High Involvement Management,* (San Francisco: Jossey-Bass, 1983).

Lawler's book is an excellent critique of the many participative management approaches that are popular in North

America today. He explains each approach in detail, and describes the strengths and weaknesses of each. Finally, he presents a model for implementing participative management through integration of the best of current approaches.

Mills, Quinn. *Rebirth of the Corporation* (New York: Wiley, 1991).

This new publication has many excellent examples of attempts to and successes of implementing some of the principles of participative management. We particularly liked the inclusion of comments by the participants in some of the projects. So often the consultants interpret what people say, and we felt this approach was effective.

Mills introduces a concept of "clusters" as opposed to teams. Clusters represent an enlarged sphere of influence around issues and is an answer to increasing the effectiveness of natural work groups. He makes the point that the traditional concept of teams made up of six to eight highly interconnected people is only one method of organization. This supports our description of types of teams in Chapter 4. This easy-to-read book is useful for expanding the concept of organization effectiveness.

Weisbord, Marvin R. *Productive Workplaces,* (San Francisco: Jossey-Bass, 1987).

Weisbord wrote this book, we believe, as a motion picture of a journey. He begins with a depiction of the origins of management theory and how it has changed from the days of Frederick Taylor to today, and takes it into the future. He provides guidelines for increasing participation of all levels of the organization in the improvement of whole systems rather than the traditional approach of relying on experts to provide the "right" answers.

INDEX